KIVA ART OF THE ANASAZI AT POT
E 99 P9H46
A00978591001

D1775412

KIVA ART OF THE ANASAZI

KIVA ART OF THE ANASAZI

at Pottery Mound

by Frank C. Hibben

KC PUBLICATIONS / LAS VEGAS, NEVADA

Book Design by K. C. DenDooven

Edited by Gwen DenDooven

First Edition. First printing, October 1975

Library of Congress Number: 75-19742

ISBN 0-916122-16-6

KC Publications, Box 14883
Las Vegas, Nevada 89114

© 1975 by Frank C. Hibben. All rights reserved.

   No part of this book may be reproduced in any form or by any means without permission from the publisher, except by a reviewer who may quote brief passages.

Printed in the United States of America

THIS BOOK
IS AFFECTIONATELY DEDICATED
TO
THE LATE MRS. HARRIET (HATTIE) COSGROVE,
THE LATE MR. W. S. (PA) FULTON,
AND
THE LATE MRS. W. S. (ROSE) FULTON,
THE MOST BELOVED AND RESPECTED FIGURES
IN ALL OF AMERICAN ARCHEOLOGY.

Contents

INTRODUCTION

I — Discoveries

- 2 Discoveries
- 12 Pottery Mound Kivas
- 14 Removal of the Murals
- 16 Destruction and Defacement
- 18 Kiva Construction
- 24 Physical Aspects of the Frescoes
- 28 Renewals of Plaster Coats
- 36 Paints Used in the Murals
- 49 Pigment Binder and Vehicle

II — Kiva Art

- 54 Kiva Art
- 59 Mexican Influences
- 67 Abstract Designs

74	Medallions
78	Human Figures
88	The Mystery of the "Spanish Priest"
93	Birds and Feathers
102	Prayer Sticks and Tiponis
107	Mammals
113	Snakes and Reptiles
115	Insects
117	Zoomorphs
118	Spirit Figures
120	Textiles
126	Baskets
130	Shields
134	Stars
134	Rainbows
136	Clouds and Lightning
138	CONCLUSION
139	BIBLIOGRAPHY
141	KIVA INDEX
142	FIGURE INDEX
143	GENERAL INDEX

Acknowledgments

THE WORK AT POTTERY MOUND was the result of the combined efforts of many hundreds of dedicated people, foremost among whom were the many students who labored long in the hot sun to make these results possible.

During the seasons of 1958 and 1959, the removal of the mural frescoes was aided by a series of grants from the Research Committee of the University of New Mexico. During the 1960 and 1961 seasons, the removal of the paintings from the last kivas was made possible by generous grants from the National Science Foundation. With the assistance of these grants, the technical processes for the removal of the paintings were greatly improved.

The author is especially beholden to the many members of the staff at the University of New Mexico who kindly contributed aid in their fields, particularly Dr. John Clark, former chairman of the Department of Chemistry, who donated his time and talents to the chemical analyses of paint samples obtained from the murals, and Dr. Florence Ellis, who used her intimate knowledge of dendrochronology in dating the wood specimens.

The author is also deeply grateful to his several field assistants who gave of their time and efforts over and above the requirements of their jobs. Charles Voll and Russell Schorsch worked on the pottery; Natalie Vytlacil assumed much of the responsibility for the removal of the paintings; Nora Chino from Acoma aided greatly in the laborious work of removing the paintings; Octavio Romano was in charge of the meticulous copying of the paintings on a grid system; Nancy Atkins and Tom Bahti were responsible for most of the reproductions of the paintings appearing in the color plates herein. These are but a few of the outstanding stalwarts who worked so hard to put this account together.

Not the least among them was the author's wife, Brownie Hibben, who spent many days in the field and in the preparation of the preliminary data.

Gwen DenDooven accomplished a tremendous task in editing and compiling all of the preliminary data into a finished manuscript to accompany the murals.

Mr. Byron Harvey, of the Harvey Foundation, Mr. and Mrs. Art Quinn, Mr. and Mrs. Don Kirby, and Mr. and Mrs. Joseph W. Hibben aided greatly with generous grants toward publication costs. Mr. and Mrs. Ian Henderson, Mr. and Mrs. Harry Coombs, and Mrs. Tom Husband also donated generously toward this end.

Introduction

EVERY GREAT CIVILIZATION has developed a distinctive artistic tradition. Chinese, Arabic, ancient Egyptian, and even Mayan art is known to expert and layman alike by the thousands of examples which have been preserved and displayed in museums and reproduced in publications.

One of the highly developed civilizations of the New World is the Puebloan, or *Anasazi* (a Navajo word meaning "ancient ones"). Reaching its peak in the thirteenth century, the Anasazi civilization numbered tens of thousands of people living in hundreds of stone and adobe towns. When Coronado marched up the Rio Grande in 1540, he found nearly seventy-five Anasazi inhabited towns. Of these, only about twenty-three are still occupied, some continuously since that time.

The Anasazi developed neither a glyphic system of writing nor a central government, but in all other respects they qualify as a great civilization. Especially remarkable is the rich and varied Anasazi development in religious rites centered around agriculture and the *katsina* (popularly *kachina*) *cult*, a basis of ceremonialism involving the use of effigies and rituals for the purpose of invoking the help of the spirits.

Elements of this elaborate and extensive art are used today by the Navajo, who derived from the Anasazi rich traditions of textile weaving and sandpainting. The Navajo, a nomadic tribe, moved from the north into Anasazi territory a few centuries ago and, by proximity and contact, acquired much from their culture. They adopted little, however, of the Anasazi ritual and symbolism having to do with agriculture, since the maize-growing and pottery-making activities of the Anasazi did not exert any great appeal to the wandering Navajo.

Until the excavation of ancient Pueblo sites, such as the ones at Awatovi and Pottery Mound, and the discoveries of the kivas and the exquisite paintings adorning their walls, little of the prehistoric art forms of the Anasazi had been known, and almost nothing was known of prehistoric Anasazi weaving (Kent 1957). Until these paintings came to light, the association between Anasazi and Navajo art forms was not definitely known. And of the kachina cult of 500 years in the past, at a time when many busy Anasazi pueblos dotted much of the Southwest, no significant finds in the form of ceremonial art or sculpture had been unearthed.

The term *Anasazi* now applies to all of the prehistoric peoples who lived in the plateau area of the Southwest (parts of New Mexico, Colorado, Utah, Arizona, and eastern Nevada). This plateau area was a vast expanse of terrain at an elevation higher than most of the surrounding area, but it contained many gorges, mesas, prairies, and mountains (Wormington 1947).

Present-day Pueblos live in Arizona and New Mexico. They are divided geographically into two groups—the western Pueblos (Hopi and Zuni), and the eastern Pueblos in the Rio Grande drainage (Taos, Picuris, San Juan, Pojoaque, Nambe, Jemez, Tesuque, Santa Clara, San Ildefonso, Zia, Cochiti, Santo Domingo, San Felipe, Santa Ana, Sandia, Acoma, Laguna, and Isleta) (Bahti 1968). These are the descendents of the prehistoric Pueblos (Anasazi), who succeeded the Basketmakers, an even more ancient people dating from about the birth of Christ to A.D. 700. (Dates for the periods of the Pueblo culture are given in table 1, page 4.)

By late Basketmaker times, these hardy people had developed an agricultural system and had begun to build permanent structures in which to live and store their corn. The Pueblos became even more accomplished at farming than their Basketmaker ancestors. They were also highly skilled in construction and built huge communal structures—the pueblos by which they are now known. The Spanish conquistadores found the Anasazi living in these apartment-house forts when they first came into the plateau area of the Southwest in search of treasure and adventure.

A second major culture, or way of life, in the ancient Southwest was the *Hohokam* (a Pima word meaning "those who have vanished"), who lived in the lower elevations of central and southern Arizona and adjacent parts of Old Mexico. The Hohokam also were farmers, but they lived for the most part in semisubterranean pithouses covered over with poles and dirt. The Hohokam had different traditions and languages from the Anasazi, and their pottery, like most of the other things they manufactured, was distinct. Pottery Mound is not of the Hohokam tradition; however, these people are mentioned here because of the interesting fact that the Hohokam constructed ball courts in the Mexican manner and occasionally built flat-topped pyramids—features also appearing at Pottery Mound. Perhaps some Mexican influences came to the Anasazi via the Hohokam.

The series of mural frescoes with which this work is concerned is from the site known as Pottery Mound, a Pueblo community which thrived from about A.D. 1300 to 1475. The paintings adorned the walls of the seventeen excavated kivas. An integral part of ancient (and modern) Anasazi ritual, kivas invariably are found in connection with Anasazi remains. Kivas are round or square, usually subterranean rooms entered by means of a ladder placed through a hatchway in the roof. The kiva was called an *estufa* (oven) by the Spanish because it was so hot and stuffy. The kiva of Pueblo times undoubtedly grew out of the Basketmaker pithouse, also entered through the roof.

In order to make the interior of the kiva more comfortable and to allow smoke to escape, the Anasazi very early developed a ventilator system. A shaft was drilled straight down outside the kiva wall, then turned at right angles to enter the kiva at floor level. Cold air was sucked down this shaft as the hot air from the central fireplace and the smoke moved out through the hatch in the roof. So that the cold draft would not gutter the fire, a vertical slab of stone, or "deflector," was placed between the ventilator shaft and the firepit. All kiva accouterments had a ceremonial significance—even the ventilating shaft, deflector, and firepit—and they were usually placed near the south or east wall of the kiva. Toward the opposite, or north wall, a round opening led down through the floor. This was the *sipapu*, or spirit entrance to the lower world.

This volume deals almost entirely with the murals from the kivas of Pottery Mound, the dating of the paintings, and other circumstances pertaining directly to the murals. Its primary purpose is to present these paintings to the world. Explorations of the ethnological, ritualistic, and artistic content of the paintings will be left to scholars whose expertise lies in those fields, and it will undoubtedly take many years for them to draw reliable conclusions from this wealth of material. It is indeed fortunate that, with this rare opportunity to see and examine these remarkable works of long-dead and nameless artists, such studies can now be pursued.

As for the many details of architecture, burials, ceramics, and other data from Pottery Mound, these will be the subjects of future publications. Meanwhile, all of these data are on record and available at the Department of Anthropology, University of New Mexico. Two ceramic studies of Pottery Mound material have already been made. Mr. Charles Voll, now of the National Park Service, did an intensive study of the Pottery Mound glaze-paint pottery, which aided greatly in the dating of the paintings. Russell Schorsch later did another ceramic study, which corroborated the work of Mr. Voll.

The paintings discovered at Pottery Mound constitute the most extensive body of kiva art ever brought to light, an art form which is probably the earliest found within the boundaries of the United States, except for petroglyphs and pictographs. Of the over 800 prehispanic mural frescoes unearthed to date at the site of Pottery Mound, New Mexico, 109 of the most complete are reproduced here for the purpose of making them available for study and appreciation by scholars, scientists, artists, and laymen who are interested in Indian art and culture. The masterpieces these ancient people created at this site long ago are our best record so far of Anasazi art and religion, and as such are a priceless heritage from one of the great civilizations of the North American continent and the world.

I – Discoveries

Fig. 1. This figure dressed as a bird may be performing the bird dance. The "kiva-step" design above is symbolic of rain clouds. (KIVA 7, LAYER 33, SOUTH WALL)

Discoveries

THE RUIN KNOWN AS POTTERY MOUND has been known for almost a century as a most unusual site, not only for its extraordinary height (about twenty-five feet above the level of the surrounding floodplain), but also for the proliferation of pottery which virtually covered the surface of the mound, giving the site its name. Such an accumulated mass of earth, sand, and debris indicated structures of several stories in height, a series of structures, or a pueblo built on a high terrace or some other elevation. Over ninety percent of the pottery found there was decorated, not utilitarian, an indication that the site had been used as a ceremonial center and would therefore contain artifacts of great significance.

Pottery Mound lies in central New Mexico, in the valley of the Puerco River, a major tributary of the Rio Grande. The Puerco Valley belongs geographically to the Rio Grande drainage, and in its major aspects Pottery Mound is recognized by archeologists as a Rio Grande, or eastern, pueblo typical of Pueblo IV date. During most of its existence Pottery Mound was closely affiliated with Rio Grande pueblos such as Kuaua, Puarai, Paako, and Galisteo, but one important difference is that the Pottery Mound site has produced evidence of many Mexican influences.

Table 2, which has been carefully worked out with thousands of tree-ring dates, indicates that glaze-painted pottery first appeared in the Rio Grande area by A.D. 1300. The glaze-painting of pottery originated there, possibly at Pottery Mound itself. This first glaze is called "Glaze I," and a typical example is the bowl in figure 4. Most Rio Grande and Galisteo sites showed sherd counts overwhelmingly Glaze III and Glaze IV. Pottery Mound, on the other hand, lies almost entirely within the Glaze I period. Little Colorado wares and Hopi types of the same dates are also fairly common at Pottery Mound.

Although Glaze III and later types of sherds were almost completely absent from Pottery Mound itself, late glazes *were* found at a small pueblo of twenty-four rooms which formerly lay on the brink of the Rio Puerco cutbank just north of Pottery Mound. This

Fig. 2. Typical framing device separates a dancing Anasazi maiden from two bird-like zoomorphs. (KIVA 2, LAYER 4, SOUTH WALL)

outlying pueblo was completely obliterated by the floods of 1956 and 1957, but was fortunately tested before its demise. It was in this vicinity that Bruce Ellis of the Museum of New Mexico, during an earlier reconnaissance, recovered a fragment of chain mail assumed to be of Spanish origin (Ellis 1956). With these exceptions, the site of Pottery Mound seems to have terminated well before Glaze III times, or about A.D. 1475. Many of the other sites in the Rio Grande province were still occupied during the Coronado entrada of 1540-41 (Vivian 1964), but there is no mention of an occupied pueblo in the Puerco area in the journals of the Spaniards.

At Pottery Mound itself, the expectation was strong that a Pueblo III pueblo had formed the basis for several Glaze I, or early Pueblo IV, structures. However, several sessions of excavation in the lowermost levels revealed that the first structure at the site was not a pueblo at all, but an artificial, flat-topped mound, with three or four levels of early Pueblo IV date superimposed upon it. A very complicated architectural history at Pottery Mound seems to have been compressed into a remarkably short period of time.

The excavations carried on here between 1954 and 1962 by the University of New Mexico Field School revealed many features not typical of Rio Grande sites—features unexpected in the area. Most important, and dramatic, of these were the discovery of the pyramid built in the Mexican manner and a series of prehistoric paintings decorating the walls of seventeen subterranean kivas.

The flat-topped structure had been pitted, modified, and dug into by later additions. The fact that the first room tiers were built on several levels is in itself suggestive of an early culture. Excavation plans for the whole structure originally included only limited

Table 1. The periods (simplified) into which most Southwest archeologists divide the prehistory of the Pueblo culture.

Period	Dates (approximate)
Basketmaker I	Birth of Christ
Basketmaker II	Early Christian Era
Basketmaker III	A.D. 100 to 700
Pueblo I & II (Developmental)	A.D. 700 to 1100
Pueblo III (Classic)	A.D. 1050 to 1300
(Also known as the "Golden Age," this period saw the greatest extension of the Anasazi.)	
Pueblo IV (Regressive)	A.D. 1300 to 1540
Pueblo V (Historic)	A.D. 1540 to Present

Table 2. Rio Grande glazeware periods (compiled as a result of the Eighth Ceramic Conference held at Santa Fe in 1966).

Glaze	Dates
I (A)	1300-1475
II (B)	Centers on 1425
III (C)	Centers on 1450
IV (D)	Centers on 1490
V (E)	Centers on 1515
VI (F)	1600 and a short period thereafter

Fig. 3. Rack containing pottery vessel, feathered baton, and other ceremonial gear. (KIVA 7, LAYER 34, SOUTH WALL)

Fig. 4. Dancer with eagle-clawed feet holds a pottery bowl on his knee. (KIVA 10, LAYER 31, SOUTH WALL)

Kiva 1, looking east. Students are working on various aspects of the paintings, and an artist is reproducing a painting from the east wall (fig. 72, p. 115). Ventilator shaft, deflector, and firepits are shown in the center of the photograph. Note the flag floor and the suggestion of a banquette on the north wall.

testing in selected areas. When it became suspected that an artificial structure might be the basis for the entire sequence, some twenty tests of small areas were carried down through the several architectural levels to examine the structure beneath. These tests were generally inconclusive, for several reasons. The various architectural levels bore no relationship to each other in plan. Furthermore, the first architectural level was built on top of the flat-topped structure beneath, and a number of trash pits and kivas were dug into it. Tests of small areas gave little information.

To resolve these uncertainties, in 1961 the southern edge of this structure was laid bare. The resultant trench was deep enough to reveal a complete cross-section of all levels of the site, which verified that the first structure at Pottery Mound was indeed a flat-topped pyramid in two levels. The second, or uppermost, terrace of the mound was difficult to locate because later kivas, rooms, and trash pits had marred its outline, but in size it appeared to be about 215 feet (65 m.) square. The whole flat-topped structure was oriented close to north and south.

At the northwest corner of the main mound, three lower steps and slurred evidence of higher treads indicated that a stair ascended to the first level at that point. The tread of each step was about 24 inches (61 cm.) wide, with 12-inch (30 cm.) risers.

Architecturally Pottery Mound consisted of adobe-walled rooms surrounding four large plazas, in a plan usual at Pueblo IV sites. Including several additions, the structures covered approximately seven

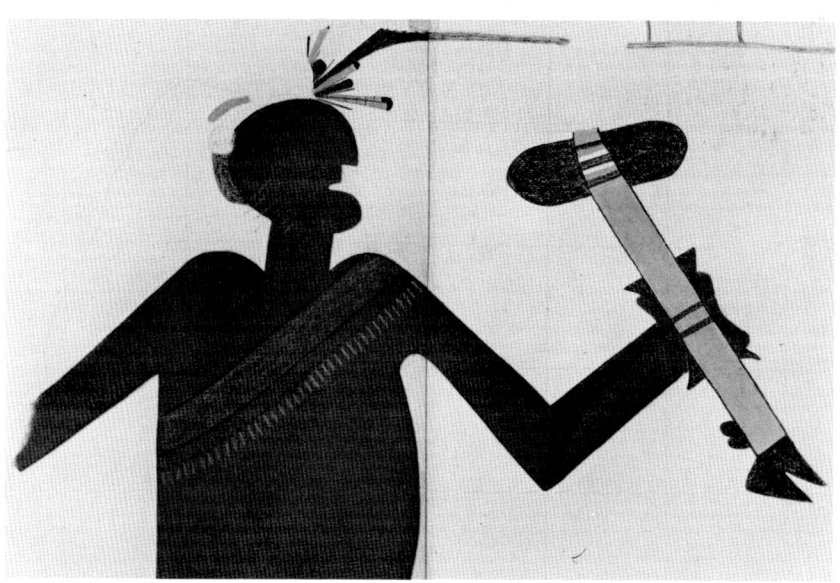

Student artist is reproducing a figure of a warrior bearing a shield (fig. 101, p. 130). A grid system was used by the artists so as to ensure absolute accuracy in measurements and proportion. A color scale was used to also ensure maximum accuracy in reproducing the colors of the murals.

Overview of the Pottery Mound site during excavations. The tent in the background covers a painted kiva, protecting it from the drying effects of sunlight and air.

This warrior with bandoleer and club (Kiva 9, layer 12) is an artist's sketch made on the grid system with colors matching those of the original mural.

acres. During the 175-year period of the active life of the site, three or four multi-roomed adobe pueblos were built. In several sections the buildings were three or four stories high. Some of the rooms within the pueblos were built on top of others in a seemingly haphazard fashion, the historical sequence of which has yet to be fully determined, i.e., room tiers had been burned or otherwise reduced to rubble and at later times other rooms were built on top of them.

The base upon which the original pyramid was built was difficult to determine. The entire substructure was a wide, low, flat mound with sloping sides, made of puddled adobe and trash fill, with a surface of smoothed caliche (a limey soil found in deserts of the Southwest). The overall height was 13 feet (4 m.). If any features were originally on the summit of the pyramid, they either have not yet been revealed or were obliterated by later additions.

The adoption of flat-topped pyramids by the Anasazi people does not seem so strange in light of the great influence exerted on many early American cultures by the type of ceremonialism indicated by such a structure. Flat-topped mounds are distributed from Aztatlan in Wisconsin to the Andean area of South America. With similar influences and structures permeating Arizona, it would have been strange indeed if the Anasazi had remained untouched. Flat-topped structures at Casas Grandes, Chihuahua, in northern Mexico, are of earth and stone and vary in shape from a plain, flat-topped mound ascended by a flight of stairs to one of cruciform (cross-shaped) plan. The flat-topped structure found at Pottery Mound is, then, simply a northern extension of this type of ritual architecture.

The time period in which Mexican influences moved northward is hard to determine, but it undoubtedly continued over a period of several centuries. Schroeder (1965) sees diffusion of Mexican traits into the Southwest prior to A.D. 700. A flat-topped structure at Gila Bend, Arizona, has been placed in the Sacaton phase of the Hohokam, which dates in that region from A.D. 900 to 1150 (Wasley 1960). Macaws, a species of parrot the Anasazi and other pueblos certainly obtained from Mexico, were buried ceremonially at Wupatki, in northeastern Arizona, about A.D. 1100. Flat-topped mounds at Casas Grandes probably date around A.D. 1225. The earliest temple mounds of the Mississippi Valley may be dated at A.D. 800.

In characteristics other than the strong Mexican influences, Pottery Mound was a typical town of Rio Grande Puebloan affiliations, one of several large pueblos built in the central Rio Grande area when a massive population influx occurred near the beginning of the fourteenth century. Chronological and cultural studies of the site are still going on, of course, but some major facts are known.

The flat-topped structure at Pottery Mound dates, from available evidence, at the beginning of the Pueblo IV period, possibly even earlier. Fourteen sherds recovered in a test within the body of the artificial structure were all of Glaze I type. However, the kivas and rooms built on top of the pyramid, and in some cases into its sides, were also of Glaze I date, and

Fig. 5. Eagle and mountain lion (?) hover over a tiponi. (KIVA 7, LAYER 9, WEST WALL)

Glaze I is the date of the first, second, third, and perhaps even the fourth of the periods of architectural construction superimposed upon the platform. If we accept outside dates of 1300-1475 for the Glaze I period (table 2), a very constricted period is left to cover the building of the mound, its abandonment, and the subsequent superimposition of three or four architectural periods. Also, the surface of the flat-topped structure was pitted and dug into, and it shows signs of erosion. All these factors support the theory that the pyramid itself may have been built prior to the Glaze I period, i.e., that it may have been of Pueblo III date.

Tree-ring dates determined from studies of specimens from Pottery Mound conducted by Dr. Florence Ellis corroborated this dating. The specimens obtained, however, were generally unsatisfactory. Of 318 wood specimens recovered from the site, all but six were of juniper and cottonwood, species usually unsuitable for dating. No actual bark or cutting dates were determined by Dr. Ellis. The most reliable dates were those following.

    Specimen 82:   Kiva 6, pine, V1411
    Specimen 83:   Kiva 6, pine, V1427
    Specimen 116: Trash near Kiva 10, pinyon, V1418
    Specimen 222: Trash in fill on pyramid, pinyon, V1381

The V preceding each date indicates that the final or cutting ring is not present; however, in the judgment of Dr. Ellis, the dates determined are within a very few years of the actual cutting dates.

To the south of the Pottery Mound structure is another edifice, one with a sunken, caliche-covered floor of unknown dimensions. This may be a court or entrance to the structure, or possibly a ball court. (Ball courts have occurred in association with two flat-topped mounds at Casas Grandes.) The practice of renewing or enlarging pyramidal structures must have been carried north with the idea itself, as evidenced by the additions to structures in the Gila-Salt drainage at such sites as Pueblo Grande (Hayden 1940) and the several additions to the original structure at Gila Bend, Arizona. Many cases of aprons or other additions to temple mounds in the Mississippi Valley are known.

In reconstructing the history of the Pottery Mound structure, then, it would seem that the original pyramid was built on the flat floodplain of the Rio Puerco at the end of Pueblo III or the beginning of Pueblo IV times. The occupants of the Pueblo III pueblos of the Puerco Valley, especially those at the Lovelace site, may have been the original builders of Pottery Mound. A gap seems to exist between the time the Pueblo III sites were abandoned in the Puerco and the time when early glazeware people populated the valley extensively. This gap may have coincided with the period of the abandonment of the structure. Even though the pyramid was solidly made of hard-packed clay and was faced on its top and slanting sides with puddled caliche, the structure could not have remained in good repair for very many years without constant attention. It was probably already in a state of disrepair when early glazeware people built a pueblo on top of it.

The Rio Puerco Valley at the site of Pottery

Mound is wide and almost level. In the whole Puerco region there is no place where a flat-topped structure of even modest dimensions would appear more imposing than at this spot. It is easy to see why the original builders constructed a pyramid there. More difficult to explain is why later Pueblo IV occupants built their pueblo immediately on top of the pyramid, covering it completely with structures extending down the sides of the pyramid and to a considerable distance around its base. This area of the Puerco Valley may have possessed ceremonial significance at that time. In covering the original ceremonial structure with their secular buildings, the Glaze I people obviously did not intend to continue the ceremonial practices for which the original structure had been intended. The early Pueblo IV people did, however, continue their contact with those to the south, as evidenced by the kiva paintings.

The site revealed, in addition to the underlying pyramid, many evidences of ties and influences from civilizations of Old Mexico, especially from the Casas Grandes area of Chihuahua. The Anasazi probably traded with the Mexicans, absorbing ritual practices and accouterments in the process. Ceramic studies revealed very strong ties, also, with the western pueblos—especially the Zuni area of western New Mexico and eastern Arizona and the Hopi area of northern Arizona. Other material from the site strongly supports this conclusion.

No evidence was found to suggest that Pottery Mound was inhabited as late as the sixteenth century. The excavated paintings were prehispanic, and

Fig. 6. Abstract panels reminiscent of designs on Sikyatki pottery. (KIVA 10, LAYER 31, WEST WALL)

some of the earlier ones were probably made more than two centuries before the Anasazi had contact with the Spanish. Thus, in 1540, when Coronado and his Spanish soldiers marched up the Rio Grande, Pottery Mound was already only a pile of rubble.

Pottery Mound Kivas

Rio Grande pueblos, in common with other developed pueblo structures, usually feature a number of subterranean kivas, and in Pueblo IV times the kivas were usually rectangular in shape. Pueblos, both ancient and modern, are typically divided into two ceremonial halves (*moieties*), very often called *squash* and *turquoise*, or *winter* and *summer*. (The turquoise body paint on figure 7 may signify that he is of the turquoise moiety.) Marriages were allowed only between members of the separate halves. Because of the closeness of the people within their communities, the Anasazi worked out this system of exogamy, presumably to avoid problems of inbreeding. Each of the moieties possessed its own kiva, usually a large one.

In line with this, two of the seventeen excavated kivas at Pottery Mound were large moiety kivas. One of these, Kiva 10, was the only circular kiva thus far discovered at Pottery Mound and was about 22 feet (6.6 m.) in diameter. The other moiety kiva (Kiva 5) was rectangular, about 30 feet by 31 feet (8.9 m. x 9.3 m.).

The other fifteen were medicine-society kivas, and were smaller than the moieties. Medicine-society kivas cut across moiety lines; they dealt with various aspects of the ceremonial health and well-being of the entire community.

All of the Pottery Mound kivas had paintings on their walls, on varying numbers of plaster layers.

Excavations to date have uncovered approximately twenty percent of the entire site. Many more presumably "painted" kivas and other features at the site are as yet unexcavated. Work was halted in 1962 in the hope that future methods of excavation employing better tools and improved techniques of removing and preserving the original paintings would be developed. However, as this is being written, a dig at the seventeenth kiva is being conducted, an excavation made necessary in order to rescue its precious paintings from the vandalism of careless artifact-hunters. Some of the murals in this kiva have already been severely damaged by the unscrupulous and illegal activities of these people.

Although many kivas and pueblo rooms of the Pueblo III and IV periods had been excavated in the American Southwest prior to the Pottery Mound excavation, only two sites yielded any significant number of paintings. The first was the site of Kuaua, some fifteen miles north of Albuquerque in the Rio Grande Valley. Here a single painted kiva was discovered. On its walls were several layers of "painted" adobe plaster. These mural paintings were published by Dr. Bertha Dutton in 1963. The second major group of paintings and the one containing the most significant paintings prior to the Pottery Mound discoveries was found at the pueblos of Awatovi and Kawaika-a in the Hopi area (Smith 1952). These, too,

Fig. 7. Figure dances with a feathered staff. Prayer plume appears at left. (KIVA 8, LAYER 11, WEST WALL)

were on the walls of kivas. It is remarkable that so few prehispanic paintings have been recovered, when indirect evidence indicates that the painting of kiva walls was a common practice in Anasazi towns.

Removal of the Murals

A number of techniques were developed in the course of removing the paintings from the kiva walls, which themselves varied from solid adobe to a wattle-type construction supported by upright posts plastered on both sides. The rotting away of these posts rendered the walls very delicate and insecure, thus presenting great difficulties in removing and preserving the priceless paintings on their surfaces.

When the Kuaua murals were removed by technicians from the School of American Research and the University of New Mexico, a technique was worked out by which those individual layers of adobe plaster with paintings on their surfaces could be stripped from the walls and remounted on wallboard for study and display. This method gave excellent results, but it proved extremely slow and costly; and, as the paintings lost moisture, they became quite dull. Some murals faded almost entirely (Bliss 1935, 1936, 1948).

In the Pottery Mound work, a few segments of walls containing a series of paintings were removed entire to be used for exhibit purposes. Fragments of fallen walls were jacketed in plaster and moved to the laboratory for further work. The standing walls were processed in place. The kivas were covered with a large tent to keep out weather and sun and to keep the moisture in, since in each case the major problem proved to be the drying out of the wall plaster, resulting in the immediate fading of the brilliant colors of the murals. To prevent this harmful loss of moisture, walls and broken areas were capped with plaster.

As each layer of paintings was revealed, it was carefully photographed with several kinds of film to ensure maximum accuracy in recording the original colors. The paintings were copied by two artists working independently, each using a grid system to obtain exact measurements and maintain proper proportions. Extensive color notes were made to record every variation in color. After each painting was photographed and copied, it was carefully scraped from the wall to expose the plastered layer and painting beneath. These records were used in reproducing the paintings on art boards, which was meticulously done by people with a background in the field of archeology who were familiar with the original art. All this material is on file at the University of New Mexico. Figures 1 through 109 in this volume are exact reproductions of the art boards; the scale varies.

In the seventeen kivas the number of painted layers varied from three, in one of the large moiety kivas (Kiva 5), to thirty-eight, in the other moiety kiva (Kiva 10) and in medicine-society kivas 6, 7, 8, and 12. The removal of paintings was often complicated by earth fractures, intrusion of roots, and the collapse of kiva walls.

Fig. 8. These human-headed insect figures, according to Acoma informants, represent a creation scene. (KIVA 1, LAYER 1, NORTH WALL)

Table 3. Number of plaster layers and number of layers with murals in each kiva at Pottery Mound

	Plaster Layers	Layers with Murals
Kiva 1	102	6
Kiva 2	42	8
Kiva 3	Uncertain	12
Kiva 4	Uncertain	3
Kiva 5 (Moiety ?)	100	3
Kiva 6	40	38
Kiva 7	40	38
Kiva 8	40	38
Kiva 9 (Remodeled Version of Kiva 8)	10	10
Kiva 10 (Moiety ?)	40	38
Kiva 11	100+	4
Kiva 12	40	38
Kiva 13	Uncertain	Uncertain
Kiva 14	Uncertain	Uncertain
Kiva 15	44	32
Kiva 16	44	32
Kiva 17	22	14

Destruction and Defacement

One of the most interesting, and puzzling, features observed was the apparent intentional destruction of some of the paintings upon or subsequent to the abandonment of Pottery Mound near the end of the fifteenth century. In Kiva 1, for example, the north wall, which contained a creation scene (fig. 8) on its first or outermost layer, had been purposely undercut at its base and pushed forward so as to destroy the entire wall. The fragments of this wall were jacketed and taken to the laboratory for the removal of the paintings. In kivas 6 and 8 the north walls had also been destroyed, again apparently on purpose. In kivas 7 and 8 some human figures had been slashed so as to disfigure the facial features.

The paintings also showed various degrees of ancient wear, destruction, and repair. In many places segments of the plaster had fallen from the walls, carrying the paintings with them. These broken areas had been replastered with plain adobe, on which new paintings were executed. All but one of the kivas had tunnels leading through their walls to other kivas or rooms. These tunnels, in most cases, had been cut through earlier layers of paintings. In two of the kivas, alterations or additions to floors and benches covered an earlier series of paintings. The lower parts of the murals were worn away in some places where members of the kiva had sat with their backs against the walls.

In all of the painted kivas there were seven examples of graffiti superimposed on other paintings, in every instance present on the first or outermost

Figs. 9-10. Spirit masks, trailing spirals of bead strings, may represent spirits of the dead. (KIVA 2, LAYER 7, WEST WALL)

layer of fresco. Five of the graffiti were done in black paint in outline form; the remaining two were incised into the plaster. All graffiti found were heads or masked figures similar to those in the main body of paintings. Figure 17 contains such a head just above the wing of the whooping crane.

Kiva Construction

The kivas in which all of the mural paintings were discovered were constructed in a highly consistent pattern. With one exception (Kiva 10), all were rectangular, or very nearly so. A typical kiva was about 15 feet (4.4 m.) square. Inside kiva heights probably reached to about 8 feet (2.5 m.), although this is just an inferencial generality, since in only four cases were the walls preserved to roof height. The floors were covered with large slabs of laminated sandstone, carefully trimmed and matched to form a neat pavement, frequently laid on top of a layer of sand.

Roofs were built in the manner common to pueblo architecture. Heavy log beams, or *vigas*, were laid across the shorter dimension of the room; smaller sticks, or *latillas*, were placed at right angles above them. The entire framework was then covered by brush and earth. In Kiva 5, four vertical uprights with stone bases supported the roof. Charred fragments of entrance hatchways still remained in kivas 11 and 14.

An unusual feature in most of the kivas were the small passageways or tunnels through the walls. Kiva 1, 2, 6, 8, and 12 walls were originally pierced by small tunnels near the angle of the north wall, in general dimensions 24 inches high by 20 inches wide (60 cm. x 50 cm.). These led into room tiers or from one into another, as in the case of kivas 1 and 2, where the tunnel from Kiva 1 led into the southwest corner of Kiva 2. These tunnels must have served as entrances for "special effects" or a *deus ex machina* for certain ceremonies. The tunnels, though unusual, were not unique (Hibben 1937).

(In discussing kiva features and the locations of paintings, walls are referred to as, for instance, a "north" or a "west" wall, although in most cases the orientation is several degrees off the true direction. The sketch of the site on page 21 indicates the actual orientation of all the kivas.)

Eleven Pottery Mound kivas were oriented to the south. Six were oriented to the east. All kivas on the east side of the site were oriented in an easterly direction—i.e., special features such as ventilating shafts, deflectors, firepits, and altars were near or against the south walls or were near or against the east wall.

Banquettes were sometimes present on the south walls, as in Kiva 12, but they were also present on the north wall of Kiva 9 and on the east, west, and north walls of Kiva 10. Banquettes were usually high (24 in. or 60 cm.), and thus probably served as a shelf for ceremonial gear rather than as seats, although they may have been used as both.

Through the south or east walls in each case passed a horizontal air vent, its mouth placed at floor level. It was always of rectangular section, approximately 12 to 16 inches (30-40 cm.) in width by somewhat less in height, and it extended through and just beyond the wall. At that point, in all kivas in which

Fig. 11. Composite ghost figures. (KIVA 7, LAYER 30, WEST WALL)

Typical Pottery Mound kiva. This one is oriented east, with ventilator shaft, deflector, altar, and firepit toward the east. The sipapu, entrance to the lower world, is west of the firepit. Holes for loom uprights and banquette appear on the north.

this end of the room had survived, a vertical shaft rose from the tunnel to the surface of the ground. This feature is, of course, the familiar "ventilator" found in nearly all Pueblo kivas.

The three other walls were usually without any other features except the banquettes and tunnels already noted. The west wall invariably had a small niche midway between floor and ceiling. This was of oval outline and was deep enough for a human hand to place offerings there.

The Pottery Mound kivas can be compared to present-day Hopi kivas of the same type, in which an altar for ritual observations is set up near the end opposite the firepits and ventilator. Participants and spectators stand or sit in the center of the room facing the altar. It is for this reason that some authorities describe the altar end of the room as the "front" and the ventilator end as the "back."

Two Pottery Mound kivas had permanent adobe altars immediately adjacent to the firepits. In Kiva 2 a well-made altar in a "step" outline was well to the east of the center; in this case, the west would have been the front end. In Kiva 12 an adobe altar, also in a step outline, was oriented south of the center of the kiva. Fragments of paintings covered both altars.

On the west walls of various kivas, the designs were often arranged around the niches, or the niche itself formed a part of the design. The paintings were also accommodated to the tunnel entrances. In three instances the tunnels had been cut through an earlier series of paintings and then replastered.

In most cases the kivas were entirely within the

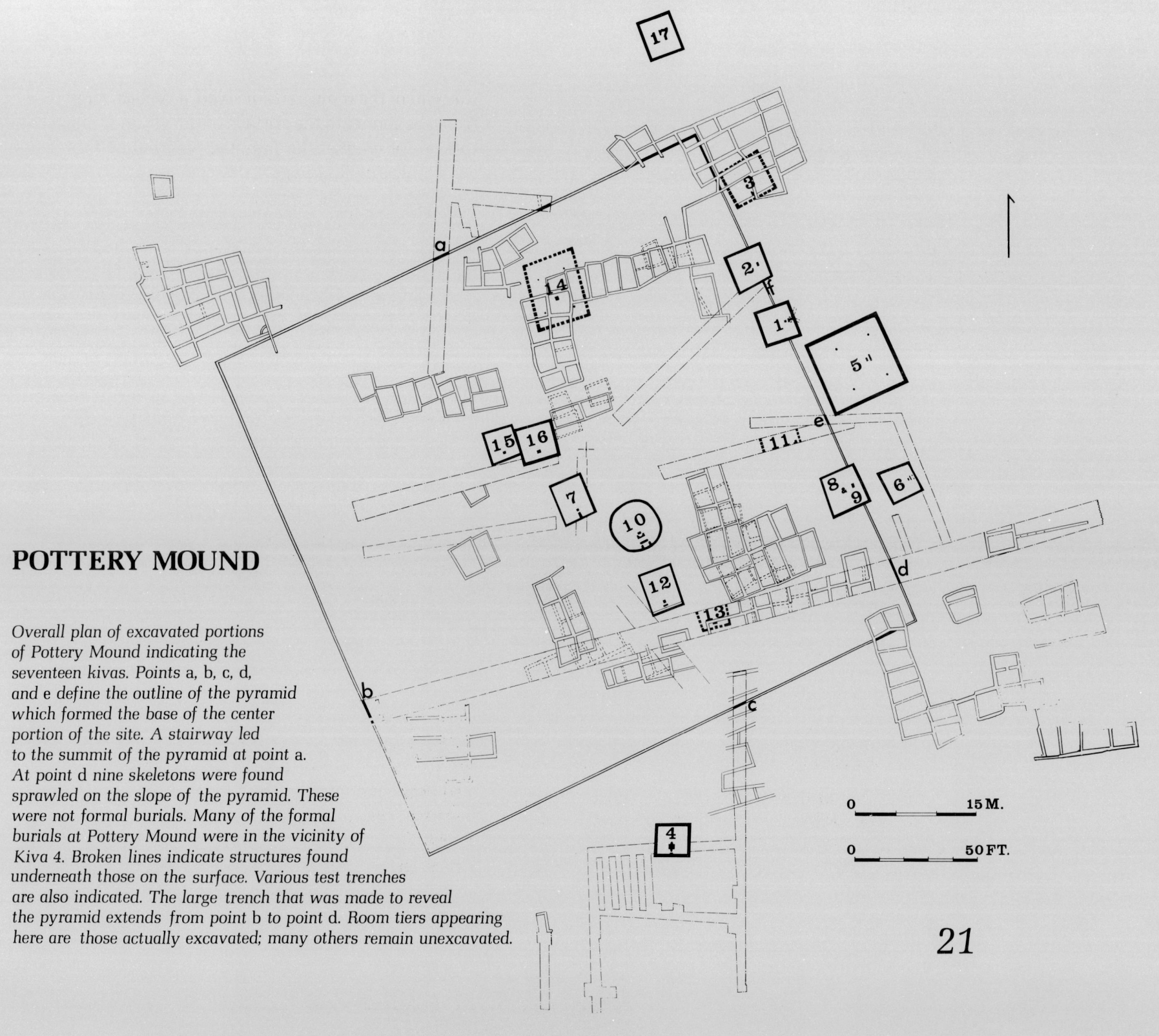

POTTERY MOUND

Overall plan of excavated portions of Pottery Mound indicating the seventeen kivas. Points a, b, c, d, and e define the outline of the pyramid which formed the base of the center portion of the site. A stairway led to the summit of the pyramid at point a. At point d nine skeletons were found sprawled on the slope of the pyramid. These were not formal burials. Many of the formal burials at Pottery Mound were in the vicinity of Kiva 4. Broken lines indicate structures found underneath those on the surface. Various test trenches are also indicated. The large trench that was made to reveal the pyramid extends from point b to point d. Room tiers appearing here are those actually excavated; many others remain unexcavated.

architectural complex of the ruin, with dwelling rooms all about them, thus making them in effect, if not literally, subterranean.

Floor features of the kivas were fairly consistent, and usually included a well-made firepit of rectangular form located in front of the ventilator opening. Five kivas had two firepits each, located close to each other in the long axis of the room. The firepits usually contained wood ashes.

Between the firepit, or pits, and the mouth of the ventilator tunnel was an upright slab of sandstone used as a draft deflector. Halfway between the firepit and the opposite wall was a small aperture in the sandstone floor intended to symbolize the *sipapu*, or entrance to the underworld. Frequently floor slabs were pierced with rows of eight to ten small circular holes, each 1.5 to 2 inches (4-5 cm.) in diameter, which may have originally served as a means of fixing pegs to anchor the lower warp beams of upright looms, or they may have served as sockets for holding upright the wooden slats and other items of paraphernalia used in the ceremonies.

The walls themselves varied from 12 inches (30 cm.) to almost twice that thick. In some kivas having many painted coats of plaster, the layers themselves made up perhaps a third of the thickness of the walls. Smoke blackening was noticeable on many paintings, especially near the tops of the walls.

Life at Pottery Mound was not static. Alterations and renovations were constantly being made in many of the kivas, although several seem to have existed throughout their lives without any major revision.

Fig. 12. Zoomorph with beak and claws holds the end of a lightning bolt decorated with a head and a feather ruff. The lightning bolt extends around a large medallion enclosing a bird.
(KIVA 8, LAYER 1, SOUTH WALL)

Some of the alterations may merely have been repairs made necessary by the partial collapse of portions of the walls. Kiva 8 is obviously an actual revision of Kiva 9.

Physical Aspects of the Frescoes

The mural frescoes of Pottery Mound varied considerably in form, changing with the purposes of the paintings and probably with the individual tastes of the ancient artists.

The murals were done on thin layers (less than three millimeters thick) of finely prepared adobe plaster. When a new painting was needed, perhaps for a certain Anasazi ceremony, a layer of adobe was plastered over the face of an existing one, and the painting was applied to the new surface. Water, and sometimes animal grease, was used as a medium. The pigments, for the most part, were mineral in origin. Some vegetable pigments were used, but these were not as enduring as mineral pigments and have largely disappeared, leaving only the outlines of areas originally colored (fig. 8).

The palette of colors used by Pottery Mound artists was exceptionally large and varied. Eight shades of red were distinguishable. Three shades of yellow, two of green, and two of blue were usual in the series. The artists often used a strong purple, a maroon, and a flaming orange. Many painted areas were outlined in black. Brushwork was exceedingly fine, as in the depiction of certain feathers, but its quality varied. Obviously a number of artists differing in ability executed the paintings over a long period of time. Shading was usual, and some colors were superimposed (fig. 24) to produce variations of effect. Incising (carving into the plaster to produce a raised, or textured, effect) was also used to add details and supplement the paint, as in the vivid designs of the kilt in figure 72 and the shirt in figure 30.

The basic background color was the light brown of the adobe plaster, but the adobe colors varied among kivas from a rich medium brown to gray. The plaster itself was finely prepared, apparently sifted so that no particle was larger than five micro-millimeters in size. The natural adobe color was a very good background for most of the murals. The paint was usually applied after the plaster had dried (*fresco secco*), but in a few instances the paint was apparently applied while the plaster was still moist, the color penetrating through the thickness of the plaster layer, perhaps unintentionally.

To heighten the contrast between painting and background, the plaster in several instances had been "whitewashed" (figs. 13, 60). This white coating, a gypsum wash, also appeared on the walls of many of the rooms at Pottery Mound, none of which contained paintings. In the painted kivas the gypsum wash, besides serving as a better background for the paintings, may also have tended to reflect light from the hatch entrance. The kivas must have been quite dark and the paintings difficult to see, especially after smoke blackening had darkened the ceiling beams and the upper portions of the walls. Apparently the Anasazi discovered, perhaps by accident, that the

Fig. 13. *Abstract panel containing, among other elements, stylized parrots.* (KIVA 1, LAYER 3, NORTH WALL)

Fig. 14. *Council of chiefs with elaborate headdresses and ceremonial spears. "Rainbow man" at right holds a bird-like scepter in his clawed hand.* (KIVA 2, LAYER 1, NORTH WALL)

whitewash provided more light in the windowless rooms.

Pottery Mound artists never used a whitewash to cover or obliterate previous paintings, as in other kivas described by Villágra (in Espinosa 1933). In obliterating a mural no longer needed, Pottery Mound artisans always simply spread a fresh layer of plaster over existing paintings and used this as a background for a new creation.

Four major methods of depiction were used in all of the paintings at Pottery Mound. The most common (used in over five hundred of the paintings recovered) involved the use of a ground line. This ground line, usually done in red, sometimes extended all the way to the bottom of the kiva wall (fig. 49). In other cases it was a narrow red band, sometimes outlined in black both above and below (fig. 15). The figure or figures either stand or sit on this ground line. Baskets, pottery, and other objects depicted were drawn in relation to the ground line (title page).

A second arrangement was done with a ground line below and cloud patterns above. Figures on the ground line sometimes extended into the cloud areas or were superimposed upon it (fig. 14).

Eighty-two of the paintings recovered employed the use of a "framing line." Consisting of rainbow bands of color, this framing line crossed the walls of the kiva in a repetitive, fret-like border. The usual arrangement was to paint the framing lines around all four walls of the kivas on the same plaster layer, so as to have two frames on each wall. The figures either stood on the framing line or were enclosed by it (fig. 16). Parrots, other birds, and objects sometimes perched or sat at the corners of the frames (fig. 18). A variation of this technique was the use of the rainbow frame in a rectangular form, enclosing a single element of the painting. Occasionally an opening was left in the frame (fig. 5).

A fourth arrangement involved no ground line and no framing line (fig. 76). Designs were placed approximately in the middle of the wall with no reference to ground or sky. In a few instances figures were placed head downward as though descending from the sky, but the sky was not shown. It was often difficult to determine what constituted a single painting. Usually a whole wall of one painted layer was one composition (fig. 17), but in many instances the artist seemed to group his figures in two or more compositions on a single wall.

Many times one motif, with or without a framing line, was carried throughout a continuous layer on all four walls of a kiva, completely enclosing it. The shield motif in figures 102, 103, and 104 (Kiva 2, layer 3) is a nearly complete example of this striking arrangement.

Renewals of Plaster Coats

Replastering kivas in the Anasazi villages was, as it is in modern pueblos, a widespread practice. Many kivas excavated in the Southwest have been reported as having been "replastered" and possessed of successive layers. Repeated renewals of plaster by superimposition of layers has been reported in a number of kivas dating from Pueblo II and later times.

Fig. 15. Rattlesnake is superimposed upon an "eagle man." (KIVA 8, LAYER 8, EAST WALL)

Table 4 indicates some of the plaster series in kivas at various sites. Again, it is remarkable that so few of these kivas had mural paintings on their walls.

Most of the multiple layers of plaster in many of the rooms at Pottery Mound could be distinguished by smoke blackening between the layers, forming a "varve." In several modern pueblos, such as those at Hopi, plaster is renewed once a year; outside adobe walls are renewed at the same time. If such had been the case at Pottery Mound, then each varve would have represented a year's occupation of a particular room. The numbers of layers of wall plaster in the various room tiers of Pottery Mound varied from one to one-hundred-plus.

Kiva walls may have been replastered to hide or obliterate previous paintings. At Pottery Mound only occasional smoke blackening or wear indicated that a particular painting had been exposed for a long period of time. Indeed, many of the Pottery Mound frescoes appeared to have been covered over only a day, or at the most several days, after they were created. The ceremonial practice of destroying or obscuring any motif used in a sacred rite was widespread in ancient times, as it is still. The art on the Pottery Mound kiva

Table 4. Various excavations of prehistoric kivas of different periods, demonstrating that the replastering of kivas was a common practice among the Anasazi.*

Site	Locality	Pueblo Period	Maximum Number of Layers	Authority
Alkali Ridge	Southeastern Utah	II	2	Brew 1946, pp. 141, 212
Tseh So	Chaco Canyon, New Mexico	II	14	Brand, Hawley, Hibben 1937, p. 77
Rattlesnake Point	New Mexico	II, III	27	Bahti 1949, p. 53; Hibben 1948
Lowry Ruin	Southwestern Colorado	III	25	Martin 1936, p. 44
Far View House	Mesa Verde, Colorado	III	40	Fewkes 1917, p. 139
Hawikuh	Western New Mexico	IV	63	Hodge 1922, p. 5
Kuaua	Near Bernalillo, New Mexico	IV	29	Vivian 1935, p. 113; Dutton 1970
Sikyatki	Hopi Country	IV	?	Fewkes 1898, p. 645
Awatovi	Hopi Country	IV	100	Smith 1952
Kawaika-a	Hopi Country	IV	25	Smith 1952

*This table was first compiled by Watson Smith (1952) and appears here with some deletions and additions.

Fig. 16. *Dancing female holding prayer plumes is flanked by dancers holding parrots.* (KIVA 2, LAYER 4, WEST WALL)

Fig. 17. *Interior kiva scene. Headdresses and strings of beads hang from a rack above. Left: Figure with shield holds a cornstalk staff. Others hold containers of ceremonial gear. Right: A married woman (hairdo) and a man with an elaborate headdress are seated on the kiva floor with a whooping crane and a basket of bead coils between them. Other strings of beads and blankets hang from the rack above. The rectangular outline in the center indicates the tunnel to Kiva 3.* (KIVA 2, LAYER 1, NORTH WALL)

walls was certainly of ceremonial significance and may well have been subject to the rules governing this custom.

Stephen (1936) recorded this practice in use among the modern Hopi when elaborate wall paintings at Walpi in 1893 were "almost entirely quite obliterated by rubbing and scraping" only two days after having been made. Reagan (1917) reported at Sia pueblo that the painted walls of a kiva had been whitewashed in order to prevent him, as he thought, from seeing the designs. This may have been the case, but it was more likely a standard ceremonial practice derived from ancient times which served to prevent "profane" eyes from seeing sacred designs. Present-day Hopi simply "explain" that wall paintings are washed off as soon as their function has been served.

A well-known example which reaches back almost into the period of Pottery Mound is the account of Oñate in 1598. In this account, as told by Villágra (in Espinosa 1933), Oñate's party reached the pueblo of Puarai in the middle Rio Grande Valley. There is some question as to the precise pueblo referred to by Villágra, but it was certainly one of the ruins in the vicinity of the modern town of Bernalillo, New Mexico, on whose surface pottery similar to that of Pottery Mound was found. As such, Pottery Mound in its last days was a contemporary of Oñate's Puarai and closely related to it culturally. Villágra related that the walls of a room in which the Spaniards were quartered had been recently whitewashed, but that the next day, when the whitewash had dried, it was possible to see the details of a mural painting beneath it.

Again, as in the case at Sia, this whitewashing was probably a ceremonial routine and not an impromptu device executed to prevent the Spaniards from seeing the paintings, as Villágra assumed.

The Navajo observe a similar practice by destroying a ceremonial sandpainting immediately after its use and before the end of the day on which it is made. It is almost certain the Navajo learned sandpainting and the rituals accompanying it from early contacts with Anasazi groups such as those at Pottery Mound. The ceremonial obliteration of sandpaintings then takes on added significance. Matthews (1902) was not satisfied as to why the Navajo destroyed their sandpaintings, but gives the explanation that "the custom of destroying these pictures at the close of the ceremonies and preserving no permanent copies of them arose, no doubt, largely from a desire to preserve the secrets of the lodge from the uninitiated." Spier (1932) reports that the Havasupai always rub out a drawing made in the sand for fear someone would use it to bring illness to the artist. Indeed, it is a common apprehension among many peoples that the "power" in an object or design may be misused by an evil antagonist ("black magic").

The Pottery Mound kiva walls were probably replastered for any or all of these reasons, but we are still without any reliable measures of time intervals between renovations and of the duration of occupancy of any given kiva. The hope that the varves between plaster layers in room tiers might be used to determine calendar periods is intriguing but unsupported. Perhaps the best answer to the puzzle of

Fig. 18. Masked dancer with a feathered staff and elaborate shell necklace. Two parrots are perched upon the corners of the frame. (KIVA 2, LAYER 11, WEST WALL)

Fig. 19. Masked spirit figure with tail, dressed as an Anasazi in a tasseled kilt. (KIVA 2, LAYER 2, EAST WALL)

the painting of murals and the subsequent covering of them is the one received by Leslie White (1932) from a priest of Acoma: "When I asked an informant why people prayed with prayer sticks, he replied, 'Cause that's the way they do.'"

Paints Used in the Murals

The paint colors used by the muralists at Pottery Mound were determined by ritual usage, psychological factors, personal embellishments, ceremonial pressures (drouth, disease, war, etc.), and of course by the materials available for making the paint.

A paint usually consists of three elements: the pigment, or coloring material; the binder, or the substance that serves to stabilize the pigment and fix it to the surface to be painted; and the vehicle, which gives to the paint a fluid character and allows it to be freely and evenly applied to a surface.

The pigments used are the most important element, since they alone provide the color, and they are the elements which can most easily be identified through analytical techniques. The range of colors found on the kiva walls of Pottery Mound included black, white, gray, yellow, blue, green, red, salmon, pink, orange, vermillion, brown, purple, lavender, and maroon. These colors occurred in many different shades, but the analyzed mineral makeup of the pigments was fairly homogeneous. The wide variations in shades were probably due to inconsistencies in mixing the elemental colors and to impurities in the materials from which they were made. As many as eight shades of red could be identified, but chemical

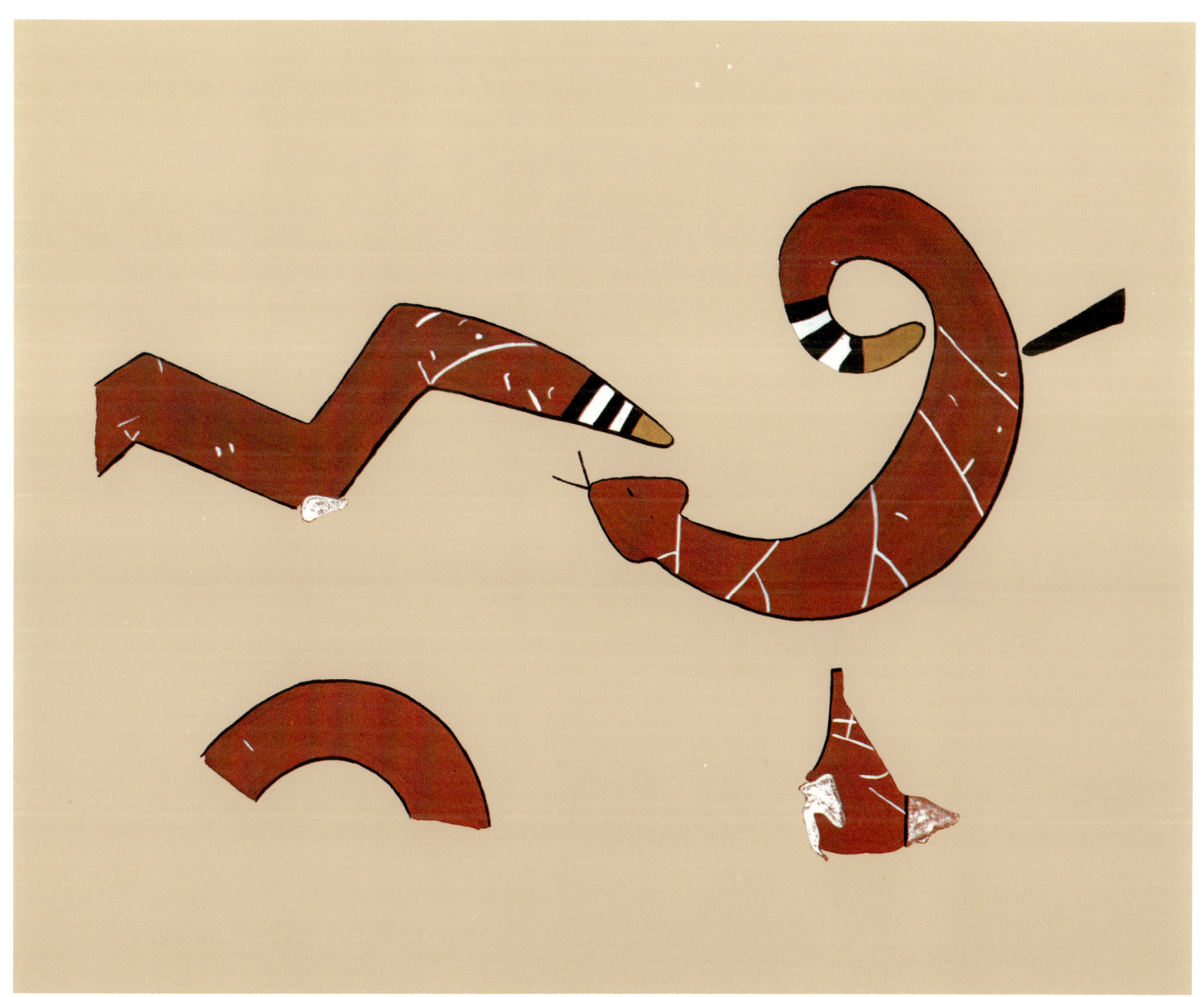

Fig. 20. Rattlesnakes, used here as rain symbols. (KIVA 10, LAYER 5, EAST WALL)

Fig. 21. Abstract panel containing stylized feathers and curvilinear elements. (KIVA 10, LAYER 4, NORTH WALL)

analyses showed that all the reds had similar or identical ingredients. Undoubtedly the many artists had different sources of clay, rock, and minerals to produce desired variations of color. Except for black and green, the pigments were apparently entirely mineral in origin.

Analytical tests were made by corroborative methods on four hundred samples. During the excavations in the fields, small samples of the plaster and scrapings from various parts of the paintings were preserved to use as guides in reproducing exact colors.

Several caches of what were probably sources of raw pigment were found. In Kiva 6, twenty-two pieces of minerals were found. These were lumps, in a variety of colors, that showed facets where powder used for paint had been scraped off. Abraded lumps like these were found in other parts of the ruin also. In all cases they were natural minerals or mineralized pieces of shale, sandstone, and clay—such as yellow ochre, red ochre, malachite, azurite, uranium oxide, and turquoise. These paint samples and raw pigments were carefully tested by the late Professor John Clark, for many years chairman of the Department of Chemistry at the University of New Mexico. Dr. Clark's analyses and comments follow, with some examples of figures in which the specific colors appeared.

Red (figs. 19, 20, 21)

The reds occurred in several shades, but all seemed to be derived from red iron-oxide of the mineral hematite (Fe_2O_3) or from clay or sandstone containing hematite. The use of hematite is corroborated

Fig. 22. Stylized panel containing parrots, feathers, and other Sikyatki-like motifs. (KIVA 16, LAYER 9, NORTH WALL)

by the discovery of numerous lumps of the raw mineral in the rooms of the ruin and in Kiva 6.

Vermillion (figs. 33, 41)

Vermillion occurred rarely and was probably an accidental variant of red caused by the mixture of red ochre with clay or silicious matter. In color it resembled closely that of cinnabar (mercuric sulphide). Only two samples tested, however, showed indications of that mineral. Other samples classed as vermillion indicated iron content.

Maroon (figs. 12)

Maroon also was widely used in the murals.

Analysis revealed in each case iron-oxides either mixed with or derived from colored clays.

Pink (figs. 22)

Pink was probably a mixture of red iron-oxide and white clay. It may have been from an indurate (hard) iron stone or from a purposeful mixture. It is also possible that the original color was not pink at all, but red (fig. 24). In many designs the muralist painted a fairly large area with a base coat, usually white, and then painted features over the base white. The superimposed colors often completely obliterated the base coat. For example, if the outer design were largely red,

Fig. 23. This dancer with fur kilt and tassels is probably not an Anasazi. (KIVA 8, LAYER 16, WEST WALL)

part of which later wore or flaked away, the resultant color would have appeared pink at the time of excavation. A scraping of the sample indicated an apparent mixture of red ochre and white clay, or silica, whereas a more correct analysis would have been pure-red ochre overlying pure-white clay, since the underlying white had originally not been visible in the finished painting. In some cases it was quite obvious that this was indeed the intention, and the colors in such instances were recorded in terms of the topmost coat. In other cases the artist placed one color over another to attain a special effect. Stippling was also used, as in figure 80.

Salmon (figs. 23)

Salmon was a definite color. In some designs this was probably a variant of the pinks and oranges. Salmon was used as a flesh color in certain figures and was also found in abstract designs. Indications of iron resulted from analysis of the pigment.

Orange (fig. 98)

In several examples a very bright orange resulted from the mixing of red and yellow iron-oxide and white clay. Another orange was achieved by stippling a yellow iron-oxide over a red layer. A common orange color contained sand grit, indicating an origin from orange sandstone containing oxide of iron.

Purple (figs. 25, 26)

Shades of purple and lavender must have surely been favorites of Pottery Mound muralists, as they occurred commonly. Zoomorphic human figures, horned serpents, and rattlesnakes were often done in

Fig. 24. Anasazi man and woman above a rainbow in what may be a marriage ceremony. A band of white circles is superimposed on the original painting. (KIVA 16, LAYER 11, EAST WALL)

Fig. 25. Dancer with a feathered kilt carries a staff decorated with feather clusters. (KIVA 8, LAYER 15, SOUTH WALL)

shades of purple. All were basically iron-oxides, apparently derived from clays. Five scrapings proved to be mixed with red iron-oxide to produce a bright purple.

Brown (figs. 30)

A relatively rare color, brown was used mostly for body painting in figures portraying people from tribes other than Anasazi. Scrapings from the face to the far right in figure 18 showed a burned iron-oxide. Other brown areas were iron-oxide toned down with carbon particles. The brown in figure 67 (possibly a Plains Indian), gave positive tests for manganese and iron and was probably a manganese dioxide-with-iron mixture. Iron carbonate also appeared, apparently a ferric carbonate—perhaps geothite with clay.

Yellow (figs. 27, 28, 29)

Yellows were present in many shades and intensities, the variations—from a light yellow to a bright gold—doubtlessly done at random and due to the character of the particular mineral each painter had available. It probably derived from goethite or limonite (Fe_2O_3-n H_2O) or from clay or sandstone stained with these minerals. A much-used bright yellow proved to be uranium oxide (UO_2). The origin of this was probably the deposits near modern Laguna where uranium is now being mined commercially. Examination of some twenty samples gave positive tests for iron. Pieces of yellow iron mineral recovered from the cache in Kiva 6 revealed a considerable range in color and a variety of chemicals in content. Facets (abraded surfaces) indicated that the pigments were ground from these minerals, all of which occur locally in natural deposits.

Green (figs. 31, 96)

The use of this color was rare. Only twelve samples could be saved and analyzed. Ten of these, bright grass-green, gave positive tests for copper and carbonate and were definitely identified as malachite ($CuCO_3 \cdot Cu[OH]_2$). The remaining two, dull grayish-green, gave a positive test for iron and were probably mixtures of yellow iron-oxide with copper traces and perhaps carbon. One presumably green shade was probably organic in origin. Outlines in the form of leaves and other portions of plants appear, but the pigment which once filled them has disappeared entirely (fig. 8).

Blue (figs. 32, 33)

Two distinct blue pigments were used at Pottery Mound. One, a comparatively rare color on the kiva walls, was copper carbonate ($CuCO_3$) or azurite ($2CuCO_3 \cdot Cu[OH]_2$). This was an intense, bright blue blue (fig. 33). A piece of azurite was present in the group of minerals in Kiva 6. Azurite may have been traded or brought from southern New Mexico or Arizona, as no known azurite occurs in the vicinity of Pottery Mound. The other pigment was the greenish blue produced with powdered turquoise (copper phosphate), appearing in figures 7 and 32. This was spread on the wall with a viscous vehicle—possibly pinyon resin or even animal tallow. In any case, the vehicle proved inadequate for the purpose, as only occasional flecks of turquoise remained to indicate

Fig. 26. A companion to figure 25, this dancer also has a feather-decorated staff, kilt, and elaborate body-painting, including a star. (KIVA 8, LAYER 15, SOUTH WALL)

Fig. 27. Two figures with elaborate face-paint are addressed by a spirit being and two birds coming from above. (KIVA 7, LAYER 3, WEST WALL)

Fig. 28. Human figure carrying a shield, bow, and arrows is combined with the body of a mountain lion. (KIVA 8, LAYER 4, WEST WALL)

Fig. 29. *Unmarried girl (hairdo) with a mask carries coiled baskets.* (KIVA 7, LAYER 18, SW CORNER)

Fig. 30. *Dancer dressed in a kilt and an unusual checkered shirt.* (KIVA 7, LAYER 31, SE CORNER)

Fig. 31. *Composite head with feather plumes and elaborate necklace, identified by the Acoma as a "squash head."* (KIVA 2, LAYER 4, SOUTH WALL)

45

Fig. 32. Shield with elaborate feather edging, within which is a second shield with feather border, is held by a human figure also carrying a bow and arrow. (KIVA 8, LAYER 14, WEST WALL)

that the artist intended the area to be blue. The turquoise was close to the variety from the Cerillos Mines near Santa Fe and was probably derived from that source.

Blue gray (figs. 34, 35)

Much of the blue pigment was actually a dark gray-blue. It seems fairly certain, however, that in most cases the painters intended a blue color. Samples of blue gray tested revealed a mixture of carbon with silver-white silicious material of gypsum clay, a mixture common in the Puerco Valley. Some dense, hard clay lumps exactly the same color as most of the blue paint samples were found in the rooms of the ruin. Several of these were analyzed. They showed facets where powder had been rubbed off, producing a pigment identical with the blue-gray paint samples scraped from the murals. These clay lumps were formed of carbonaceous matter mixed with clay in a water-deposited bed. Clays of this consistency and color occur in the badlands of the Puerco River.

Black (figs. 37)

The use of black was very common, but the constituents from which the pigment was made varied greatly. Most of the samples tested proved to contain some form of carbon, although it was not always possible to determine its original source. A few examples were charcoal; in these, fragments of a woody structure were visible under the microscope. Two samples were bone black and gave positive tests for phosphate. Two samples were identifiable as manganese with a mixture of carbon—possibly coal. One scraping contained iron plus organic carbon.

Fig. 33. Framed bear (?) with a wig-like head covering. (KIVA 2, LAYER 9 OR 10, SOUTH WALL)

Fig. 34. Horned and plumed serpent upon which a superimposed star "soul face" appears. (KIVA 7, LAYER 9, WEST WALL)

White (figs. 37)

White pigments also were derived from many sources and consisted chiefly of silicious clay, kaolin, or a combination of both. The best source would undoubtedly have been the white, sandy clay of the Puerco Valley. Four samples contained silica and gypsum, also probably derived from natural deposits. Sixteen samples were positive for both calcium and carbonate and were thus identifiable as chalk. Several lumps of white material were recovered from Kiva 6 and the room tiers. Kaolin, with varying proportions of fine silica-sand intermixed, was the most common. Chalk or calcium carbonate ($CaCO_3$) and gypsum ($CaSO_4 \cdot 2H_2O$) were also represented by pieces of raw material.

In some instances, as in the headdresses in figures 14 (far left) and 59, sheets of selenite or crystalline gypsum were applied to the wall. This must have originally presented a glittering effect in the finished painting. With the passing of so many years and the collection of moisture in the fill, however, the selenite became amorphous and chalky. Also, the breakdown of the binding medium caused the sheets of selenite to tend to separate from the plastered wall.

Gray (figs. 36)

In many figures the dark-colored areas were gray rather than black. Painted areas that now appear gray may originally have been black, or they may have been intended as dark blue and were formed by a mixture of black and white. Whatever their original conditions and sources, the gray areas were composed of mixtures of white and black particles.

Although chemical constituents present in the pigment materials were oxides and carbonates of iron, manganese, and copper, it is amazing to note the variety of elements used by the resourceful Anasazi artists, as revealed through Dr. Clark's spectographic analyses. His completed list is as follows: major constituents: silicon, magnesium, aluminum, iron, titanium, calcium, potassium, manganese, copper, lead, and uranium; minor constituents: vanadium, chromium, barium, strontium, sodium, potassium, and molybdenum; traces: tungsten, zirconium, and others.

The colors as they appear in this volume are as close to those of the original murals as modern reproduction methods will allow. The background color, however, is uniform, even though the adobe walls did vary in color.

Pigment Binder and Vehicle

Because of the passing of so many centuries and the leaching effect of ground water, little evidence remained of the binder, the material which held the pigment to the adobe walls, but it was almost certainly organic. In the chemical analysis, several of the pigment specimens—especially black—revealed traces of phosphate, which may indicate that the binder was of animal origin. The binder probably came from several sources. Bear tallow may have been a likely candidate, except that the Anasazi, as do most modern Pueblos, probably had a ceremonial aversion to bears and treated them with great awe and reverence. (Bears, however, were depicted on several of the Pottery Mound murals.) Other fats and oils of animal

Fig. 35. Portion of large panel, containing curvilinear elements and multipointed stars. (KIVA 7, LAYER 18, SOUTH WALL)

Fig. 36. *Portion of an abstract panel revealing complicated elements reminiscent of Sikyatki pottery.* (KIVA 7, LAYER 30, SW CORNER)

origin, as well as the yolks and whites of bird eggs, may have been used as binders.

Resins and vegetable juices have also served in this capacity. A Sia informant reports that paint used on adobe surfaces is mixed with the sap of the pinyon tree gathered in the spring of the year before it becomes too thick. The sap and juices of other plants may also have served the painters of Pottery Mound as a binder vehicle. The common beeweed (*Cleome linne*) is still used by Pueblo potters as a brown paint or as a supplement to other colors "because it goes on so easily," according to an Acoma informant.

Several areas in the frescoes indicated that both binder and pigment were organic in origin, as they have disappeared entirely. In most cases the color intended was probably green, as Dr. Clark noted, since outlines left were usually leaves or plant parts (fig. 8). Chlorophyll in some form may have been used in these instances.

In most of the Pottery Mound murals, water was probably the common binder and vehicle. The surface of adobe plaster is soluble in water; pigments would thus adhere to its surface, even without a binder.

Fig. 37. *Dancer with plumed headdress and bird body. Symbolic rainclouds rise above.* (KIVA 7, LAYER 33, SOUTH WALL)

II – Kiva Art

Fig. 38. Highly stylized woman's figure wearing an elaborate headdress and a necklace with shell pendant holds two stylized parrots. Corn plants, birds, dragonflies, and other stylized elements also appear. (KIVA 7, LAYER 30, SW CORNER)

Kiva Art

ONE OF THE MAJOR BENEFITS derived from this remarkable series of mural frescoes is that it allows a rare insight into the artistic ability of the ancient and unknown Anasazi artists. So little of the art of the Anasazi has been unearthed that today's Indian artists have had few guidelines to follow; and, as some observers have pointed out, their styles are not at all similar to the work of their prehistoric ancestors. The recovery of the Pottery Mound murals will go far to fill this void and provide *all* artists and artisans with a wealth of material for use and comparison.

Some freedom of interpretation has been allowed in this publication in an attempt to make it meaningful to the general reader, but it is not the intent here to individually analyze each of the eight-hundred-plus paintings recovered from this site, even if it were possible to do so. In considering the frescoes of Pottery Mound as a whole, however, certain major elements of pattern and design stand out, and several broad inferences may be drawn with reasonable confidence.

Attempts to find relationships among various paintings, even those within the same kiva, proved generally fruitless. The smaller kivas are almost certainly medicine-society kivas, but in no instance was a connection with modern Pueblo medicine societies certain.

Pottery Mound probably belongs culturally with Laguna and Acoma. Laguna is of comparatively recent origin, but Acoma was in its present location when the Spanish explorer Oñate first described it. Testing in the refuse pit at Acoma reveals that the pueblo dates back at least to Glaze I times, and was thus a contemporary of Pottery Mound—perhaps a sister pueblo. If so, the ancient people of Pottery Mound would have spoken Keresan, as do the present-day occupants of Acoma and Laguna.

Following this assumption, a number of people from Acoma and Laguna were encouraged to view the murals as they were being excavated. Several of these people, especially the Chino family of Acoma, are privy to the esoteric rites of several of the medicine societies. (Mr. Chino has been for several years the head

Fig. 39. Dancer holding two parrots is surrounded by an "eagle man," a zoomorph with a baton, a headless eagle, and an "antelope man" (also holding a parrot). A niche in the wall appears below the principal figure. (KIVA 2, LAYER 2, WEST WALL)

of the war society at Acoma.) The Acoma all showed great interest in the murals and obviously recognized many details in them, but—perhaps because of religious reasons—they were extremely reluctant to discuss the paintings or their meanings. Some comments were extracted, however, and appear throughout this book in discussing certain of the design elements.

The Acoma did concede that the curious figures in Kiva 2, layer 8, were "direction men" (figs. 40, 41), and that similar designs are used now in certain ceremonies at Acoma. The designs within the bodies of the direction men, they said, were stylized human viscera. A single direction man guarded one of the cardinal points on each of the four walls of this kiva.

It is obvious that dozens of prehistoric artists with varying degrees of skill created the Pottery Mound paintings. Several could be identified by certain characteristics of their work. Thus, excavators of the murals were able to identify the works of the "master of the parrot ladies," who painted the charming depictions in figure 39. Likewise, the artist who did the precise paintings in figures 38 and 62 was identified as the "painter of the spotted women."

The overall quality of the Pottery Mound frescoes was excellent, even exquisite. Most of these ancient artists were extraordinarily creative, accomplished craftsmen who must have done many similar paintings previous to the ones they left behind on the kiva walls. Perhaps they practiced with sandpaintings, as small quantities of sand of various colors recovered from cracks in the kiva floors suggest. Not all

Figs. 40-41. Stylized human figures within framing devices, carrying feather-decorated staffs. Acoma informants identified them as "direction men"; each guarded a particular cardinal point. The body interiors are stylized human viscera. (KIVA 2, LAYER 8, EAST AND SOUTH WALLS)

of the Pottery Mound paintings were of that caliber, however. The scene in figure 43 reveals a definite lack of artistic skill, and the subject itself is commonplace. This depiction of a woman and child cooking food in a pot over a fire may have been done by a child.

Mexican Influences

Evidence of Mexican ceremonial influences have been found at a number of sites in the American Southwest—in the flat-topped structures and ball courts of the Hohokam area of central and southern Arizona (Schroeder 1965) and in the tiny bells and the rubber balls used on the ball courts (probably imports from Mexico). Tablitas, paint palettes, and clay figurines—all these have been recognized by various authorities as Mexican-inspired. From Mexico, too, came the custom of keeping eagles in captivity, the motif of the horned and plumed serpent (figs. 34, 42)—a favorite Mexican and Mayan theme, and the tradition of the kachina cult.

Most observers have considered the Anasazi as relatively free from direct Mexican connections. But the numerous Mexican-inspired subjects and details of the frescoes at Pottery Mound, as well as some of the architecture which lies near the center of the Puebloan development designated as Anasazi, reveal that the inhabitants must have been in close contact with some Mexican centers. They undoubtedly traded with them, absorbing ritual motifs and practices in the process, and these ceremonial usages may have spread from Pottery Mound to other Anasazi centers up and down the Rio Grande, a natural passageway

Fig. 42. A dramatic scene in which a horned and plumed serpent (with a second feather ruff) consumes a purple man. Crosses to the left are dragonflies. (KIVA 9, LAYER 8, SOUTH WALL)

Fig. 43. Crude representation of a domestic scene, perhaps drawn by a child. (KIVA 8, LAYER 5, EAST WALL)

north and south. Mexican influences have been felt in other areas less convenient. In the lower Mississippi Valley, temple mounds are associated with the designs and iconography of the southern cult, or southern death cult, which is Mexican in origin, or Mexican plus Hopewell (Baerreis 1957). And, of course, Arizona's ancient ball courts to the west of Pottery Mound attest to the Mexican or Mayan ceremonialism that took place there.

Items other than the paintings and the pyramidal substructure have been found at the Pottery Mound site which also suggest connections between the Anasazi and those to the south. Five sherds of Ramos polychrome pottery are typical of Casas Grandes in Chihuahua. A clay bell in obvious imitation of the Mexican copper form is also suggestive, and a few glycymeris, olivella, and conus shells indicate that shell trade with the south was active. But the main body of information regarding Mexican ritualistic influences upon the Anasazi at Pottery Mound is still that which is contained in their mural paintings.

One of the most common motifs of the frescoes is parrots, painted in both realistic and stylized forms. In figure 45, a typical Pottery Mound painting, a female dances with a parrot in either hand, probably macaws (*Ara macao*), a bird usually scarlet in color. This and several other paintings appear to depict live specimens. Figure 44 attests that they were live birds and not effigies, since they seem to be eating corn. Also, in figure 98, an Anasazi woman has on her back a carrying basket containing a water gourd and food, on which is perched (or tethered) a live parrot. (This is

Fig. 44. Three parrots eating cobs of corn appear within a framing device. This mural is one of the best evidences that parrots were kept in a live state at Pottery Mound. Rings of feathers may be part of parrot-training regalia. (KIVA 10, LAYER 29, EAST WALL)

the probable method by which live birds were carried from Mexico.) A further evidence that the birds were alive is the painting (fig. 46) in which a figure dances with a ring-shaped stand upon which a parrot rides.

The military macaw (*Ara militaris*), a predominantly green parrot, also is depicted in several of the frescoes, which again seems to indicate the use of live birds in Anasazi ceremonies. The thick-billed parrot (*Rhynchopsitta pachyrhyncha*) is also widely represented (figures 18, 70).

Other evidence that parrots and macaws were used in southwestern ceremonials is abundant. Their feathers were employed in the making of feather mosaics, prayer plumes, and dance costumes. Parrot and macaw feathers are greatly valued even today for use in the ceremonialism of the kachina cult. These feathers, and the plumage of other birds such as the quetzal, were described by early Mexican writers and are pictured in a number of the Mexican codices. Feather-bedecked priests played important roles in Mayan and Mexican rituals, and it is presumed that the ceremonial use of these feathers was carried northward into Anasazi territory at the same time as the tradition of the flat-topped pyramid. The scarlet macaw is found in a wild state in the tropical, or southern, portions of Mexico, while the green-colored military macaw appears much farther north, in the Sierra Madre. The thick-billed parrot has been reported as having lived in Arizona in historic times, but its normal range is well to the south of the border.

The prehistoric inhabitants of Pottery Mound must have had difficulty in obtaining birds (and con-

Fig. 45. Elaborate depiction of rainmaking ceremony in a framing device. A masked figure with the hairdo of an Anasazi maiden dances with two parrots. On her head is a pottery bowl from which a lightning bolt extends to the hand of a "mosquito man." Surrounding the figures are numerous dragonflies. Both the mosquito and the dragonfly are symbolic of rain. (KIVA 9, LAYER 2, SOUTH WALL)

Fig. 46. *A ceremony in which a figure appears carrying a live parrot on a ringed perch. Figure at far right is a spirit mask.*

sequently their feathers) from these distant sources, and the logical solution would have been to breed the birds themselves. There is ample evidence that macaws and parrots were raised in captivity not only in Mexico but also in the southwestern United States: Charles C. DiPeso, who directed the excavations at the site of Casas Grandes in Chihuahua, Mexico, found rows of adobe and stone nesting cages where macaws were kept and bred (DiPeso, 1974). At the pueblo of Wupatki, near Flagstaff, Arizona, Lyndon Hargrave found evidence not only that macaws were kept there, but that upon their deaths they were buried in a ceremonial manner (Hargrave 1933, 1970). At Pueblo Bonito, a large Anasazi site in Chaco Canyon, New Mexico, Neil M. Judd found evidence that macaws and parrots were kept in a room of the pueblo, where they were probably bred (Judd 1964). No such supporting evidence for the captivity of macaws or parrots has been found at Pottery Mound. Only a portion of the site has been excavated, however, and the implication is strong that such evidence will be found.

(KIVA 7, LAYER 10, WEST WALL)

Yet another suggestion of Mexican influence is in the figures bearing shields edged with bird feathers (figs. 101-104). Even the designs on the shields are similar to those in the *Lienzo Tlaxcala*, a codex or native book of Mexico written at the time of the Spanish conquest.

Figure 47 depicts a jaguar associated with a bird, probably an eagle; the eagle-jaguar cult of Mexico was often represented in this way. This jaguar painting was on the first, or outermost, layer in Kiva 6; other figures in the same fresco are alternate mountain lions and seated human figures (title page), many of them wearing quivers with arrows. Among the Anasazi the mountain lion was usually associated with the war society, and these figures could be councilors in a council of war. In these paintings many of the figures hold various items to their mouths. Presumably the man to the far left talks of peace, as he carries no quiver, while the figures with arrows issuing from their mouths carry quivers and talk of war. The "deer" in figure 48, also in the same kiva and layer, has a sprig of evergreen—a sign of a wish for peace and

65

prosperity—issuing from its mouth. This is remarkably similar to the usage in Mexican codices of speech scrolls to indicate meaning.

In the Pottery Mound frescoes the artists left many representations of themselves, such as those in the council of war and those in figures 14 and 17. Figure 49 also seems to be pure Anasazi, with the possible addition of a Mexican motif in the horizontal figure of a woman in the center. Mexican usage commonly depicts death or conquest by means of a shaft thrust into a figure. This dead woman with a typical Anasazi matron's hairdo appears to have such an instrument thrust into her breast.

Abstract Designs

Occurring in all of the kivas examined, and in conjunction with a bewildering array of other paintings, were a number of design panels. Thirty-five of these were recovered in whole or in part (figs. 6, 13, 21, 22, 36, 50-54). They appeared on north, east, south, and west walls and seemingly on any painted layer. In several instances the painted panel may have served as a background for a portable altar or as a supplement to other religious objects placed on the floor before it. Thus, if the abstract panel appeared on the north or south wall in a southerly-oriented kiva, it could have been an integral part of an altar complex, and the same might have been true of such a panel on the east or west wall of an easterly-oriented kiva. (It will be remembered that each of the kivas at Pottery Mound was oriented to either the south or east, i.e., the ventilator shaft, deflector, and permanent altar were

Figs. 47-48. The jaguar, the deer-like animal, and the seated human figures —together with the figures on the title-page illustration (west wall)—constitute the "Council of the Mountain Lions," described on pages 65-67. (KIVA 6, LAYER 1, EAST AND NORTH WALLS)

Fig. 49. Elaborate kiva scene. On the shelf above are headdresses and other paraphernalia. The married Anasazi woman (hairdo) is apparently dead. She is lying on an altar carried on the back of a masked priest with a feather headdress. Other human figures hold bows, quivers of arrows, a shield, a club, and staffs decorated with feathers and rattlesnakes. (KIVA 2, LAYER 1, SOUTH WALL)

close to either the south or east wall.) Some of the abstract panels, however, did not seem to conform with this regular arrangement, so it is not clearly defined whether or not the abstractions had a definite relationship to altar designs.

The design panels are rectangular in form and cover all, or almost all, of one kiva wall. Some stylized elements are recognizable as cornstalks (fig. 52) or other plants. Parrots, the most common recognizable element in such panels, and even the atlatl, an ancient hunting weapon, can be identified with ease in figure 50.

Most of the design elements in the abstract panels, however, are so highly stylized that identification of elements—clouds, plants, animals, and birds—is uncertain or impossible. The "kiva-step" design (see explanation on page 136) is still used by Pueblo artists. Other elements in the panels are pure abstractions or stylizations of ideas in the painters' minds.

Although most of the Pottery Mound murals displayed a *horuum vacui* (horror of vacant space), in no case were they overcrowded. Some of the abstractions were worked out so well in relation to the overall plan that they reveal a consummate technical skill as well as a highly developed feeling for design. Watson Smith (1952) in the case of similar abstract panels at Awatovi, notes that those designs were remarkably similar in treatment to the design elements on Sikyatki pottery, an early Hopi ware. Its common occurrence at Pottery Mound defines yet another link

Fig. 50. Stylized panel with parrots, feathers, and curvilinear elements, including a throwing stick, or atlatl. (KIVA 1, LAYER 4, NORTH WALL)

Fig. 51. Abstract panel with stylized parrots and other elements. (KIVA 16, LAYER 3, EAST WALL)

Fig. 52. Corn motif zigzags across this abstract panel. Feathers, dragonflies, and the kiva-step design indicate a preoccupation with water and rainmaking. Curvilinear elements are similar to Sikyatki designs from the Hopi area. (KIVA 9, LAYER 1, SOUTH WALL, OR SUPERIMPOSED KIVA 8, LAYER 20, SOUTH WALL)

between this site and the Hopi area of northern Arizona. Most archeologists agree that the Sikyatki style is one of the finest found among all ancient southwestern pottery types. Some modern Hopi, following the example of the famous Nampeyo (Wormington 1964), are seeking to recreate in their pottery the beautiful artistic tradition of their own ancestors.

One of the elements in figure 54 seems to represent a garden, and so perhaps this panel should not be classed as an abstraction. Of all the design panels this showed the least skill in layout and workmanship.

Medallions

Appearing at random among the frescoes was a series of medallions. They occasionally appeared in connection with other paintings; in those cases the medallion was placed toward a corner of the wall. In other instances the medallion occupied the center of the entire wall and constituted a single painting in itself.

Several of the medallions should perhaps be classed with the abstract panels; true, they are circular instead of rectangular, but the interior elements are similar. Some medallions seem to depict a cosmos or perhaps a picture of the night sky—figure 53 may be a ceremonial view of heavenly bodies. Incidentally, this particular medallion depicts stars, if indeed they are stars, in much the same way as various Mexican codices.

According to the Acoma informants, the medallion in figure 55 is "the man in the moon." The medallion in figure 56 features a small animal, possibly a skunk, with a rainbow on his back.

Fig. 53. This medallion may represent the cosmos. Spears point inward to the center. Symbols at the outer periphery may represent stars. (KIVA 7, LAYER 35, SW CORNER)

Fig. 54. Two adjoining abstract panels. The upper one contains stylized parrots (left) and curvilinear elements. The one below appears strangely incomplete or poorly laid out. Overlapping the two panels in the center is a rectangle, perhaps representing a cornfield or garden. (KIVA 6, LAYER 10, EAST WALL)

Fig. 55. This medallion, identified by the Acoma as the "man in the moon," depicts a masked warrior, with a rattlesnake headdress, carrying a quiver of arrows. (KIVA 8, LAYER 1, EAST WALL)

Fig. 56. This medallion encloses a skunk-like animal with a tiponi in its paw. A rainbow motif appears on the animal's back. (KIVA 7, LAYER 35, EAST WALL)

Human Figures

Human figures appear in most of the paintings. The Anasazi themselves are numerous and easily recognized (figs. 14, 17, 24, 49, 63), although it is sometimes difficult to pinpoint those characteristics which set them apart. The artists usually painted the skin color of their own people in light-brown or reddish tones, but these fundamental skin colors were often altered by body-painting, especially with moiety colors of yellow (*squash*) or blue (*turquoise*).

Other skin colors indicate different tribes or peoples. Thus, in figure 66, the man on the left—with the different profile and the hair style similar to that of a Mexican Indian—has a yellow body color and dark face; the man on the right—also with a different profile, and with the scalplock typical of Indians of the Mississippi area—has a white body color and dark face. (Three figures appearing elsewhere in the series also have the scalplock typical of Indians in the Upper Mississippi or Great Lakes area.) The spear-carrying Indians in figure 57 are apparently from the Great Plains; their body color is pink. It should be noted that in the latter case, as in many others, the skin color may simply indicate face- and body-painting for ceremonial purposes. The Indians in figures 23 and 67 are probably also from the Great Plains. Their headdresses display antelope and bison horns and their kilts are make of skin with hair, probably bison hide.

Many of the figures were drawn with a close eye to detail, so as to create a realistic impression. Musculature in shoulders (fig. 72) and legs (fig. 65) is well defined and occasionally exaggerated. Facial features

Fig. 57. These two figures may be either Anasazi with face-paint or Indians from the Great Plains. They carry spears decorated with spool elements and feathers; other spears appear between them. (KIVA 9, LAYER 2, NORTH WALL)

Fig. 58. Composite human figures representing, according to the Acoma, two aspects of mankind. The left figure carries a bow and arrow, and the right figure holds feathers. (KIVA 8, LAYER 6, SOUTH WALL)

are often rudimentary (fig. 65) or eliminated altogether (fig. 75).

The artists painted male and female Anasazi of varying ages, children to adults, the ages of subjects in many instances revealed by their hair styles. Thus, Pottery Mound maidens (figs. 29, 99, 100) wear butterfly hair buns gathered over their ears. (Modern unmarried Hopi maidens often dress their hair in exactly the same way.) Married matrons wear a large bun at the back of the head (figs. 17, 49). Young warriors, such as those appearing in the "Council of the Mountain Lions" (title page) wear their hair long and interbraided with colored strings of either beads or dyed cotton. Other men and women of uncertain ages wear their hair straight, long, and with little or no decoration (figs. 14, 76).

Many of the figures wear masks (figs. 18, 83), headdresses, or both. The wearing of masks is a common aspect of the kachina cult and, since the entire series of paintings is religious in nature, masked figures are to be expected. Many of the kiva wall scenes containing masked figures are possible enactments of various rituals held in that very kiva. Attempts to identify the masked figures have so far met with little success; nor have any of the masked impersonations led to a particular medicine society. A layer painted with masked kachina figures had underneath it a layer with paintings totally different in character. Face-painting is also common, and many of the human figures exhibit various styles of facial decoration (fig. 27).

The large painting in figure 49 includes a shelf,

placed above the human figures, and on this shelf are a number of spare masks and headdresses. This mural, like many others at Pottery Mound, probably portrayed items actually in the kivas when they were in use (fig. 17). Racks and shelves were suspended from the ceiling vigas and were used to store ritual paraphernalia, including many varieties of headdresses containing elaborate feather arrangements.

As for the masks and masked figures, more information may be available from a large body of data which heretofore has been very little used. (Indeed, it has not even been adequately surveyed.) These data are the thousands of petroglyphs and a much smaller number of pictographs carved and painted on rock surfaces along the Rio Puerco and on ledges and other places along the Middle Rio Grande Valley. Many contain masks or masked figures (Schaafsma 1974). The major difficulty in the study of petroglyphs and pictographs is that they are very difficult, if not impossible, to date. Fortunately, the quite precise dating of the mural frescoes of Pottery Mound should help immeasurably in future studies of these relatively untapped sources of information.

Dancers and performers often carry staffs or batons, some extremely elaborate. Feathers, rattlesnakes, and various birds are prominent in the decoration of headdresses and staffs (figs. 49, 60). The "rainbow man" in figure 14 carries in his claw-like hands a baton in the form of a bird. A similar scepter appears in figure 3.

In many instances a spear is carried in lieu of a staff. Some of these, such as those in figure 57, have

Fig. 59. This figure with dark body-paint and black face-paint wears an elaborate headdress and unusual feather earrings. (KIVA 8, LAYER 3, EAST WALL)

Fig. 60. *Dancer holds a staff decorated with a bird. At right is a feather-decorated pole, possibly an elaborate prayer plume. On the dancer's white-painted body appear black dots in various clusters, identified by the Acoma as constellations of the sky.* (KIVA 1, LAYER 1, EAST WALL)

Fig. 61. *A feather-decorated medallion is surmounted by a figure holding a feather-decorated staff. To both sides are masked figures from whose heads spring cloud and lightning symbols. Ceremonial spears separate the figures.* (KIVA 2, LAYER 13, WEST WALL)

Fig. 62. This stylized figure with elaborate necklace and shell pendant is placed near other stylized elements. The spotted body and careful style characterize the work of the artist whom excavators knew as "the painter of the spotted ladies." (KIVA 7, LAYER 30, SOUTH WALL)

Fig. 63. *Two Anasazi figures with elaborate necklaces carry plumes or banners attached to poles.* (KIVA 7, LAYER 1, WEST WALL)

Fig. 64. This figure, identified by the Acoma as a "butterfly maiden," carries a parrot and wears on her head an elaborate tablita with feathers. (KIVA 9, LAYER 1, WEST WALL, OR SUPERIMPOSED KIVA 8, LAYER 20, WEST WALL)

Fig. 65. The companion butterfly maiden also carries a parrot and wears an even more elaborate tablita and kilt. (KIVA 9, LAYER 1, WEST WALL, OR SUPERIMPOSED KIVA 8, LAYER 20, WEST WALL)

either a spool-like decoration in the middle of the spear shaft or feathers attached to the spear, or both. Others, such as the weapons carried in figures 61 and 14 were probably ceremonial spears. In the excavations at Pottery Mound four large spear points were found. All were made of selenite and were painted with red ochre. Since selenite is extremely soft and could not have served any utilitarian purpose, they were probably from ceremonial spears.

Clubs, such as the hammer-like weapon in figure 49 (far right) and in the illustration on page 7, are sometimes carried in the hands. Bows and arrows (fig. 58) and quivers (title page) are depicted in many of the murals. Those carried by dancers seem to have had only a ceremonial function; others in the hands of warriors may have been utilitarian.

Many dancers and other functionaries wear bandoleers diagonally across the chest (fig. 72 and the warrior on page 7). This parallels modern Pueblo usage in which bandoleers are worn as pure decoration, to indicate rank, or as a method of carrying substances such as tobacco, cornmeal, or ammunition. The bandoleers worn by Pottery Mound figures seem to be decorative in nature.

Arm bands and ankle bands are common (title page). These seem to be usually of dyed cotton, but some appear to be strings of shell beads and strips of animal skin. Arm bands and leg adornments are integral parts of costumes worn in various ceremonies of modern Pueblos. They also wear bells and turtle rattles on their legs and on bandoleers. Copper bells were common in Mexico, and the former inhabitants of Pottery Mound were surely familiar with them, although no real copper bells were recovered from the site.

Necklaces appear often in the paintings and are of various designs. They adorn human figures as well as the necks of zoomorphs (figs. 31, 37), animals (fig. 81), and even insects (fig. 8). The most common type of necklace is that shown in figure 63—several strands worn around the neck with a figure-8 loop attached to it and hanging down over the bosom. Another common necklace is worn by the highly stylized woman dancer in figure 62. In this type of necklace the entire neck is covered with strands terminating in the throat area in a shell (probably glycymeris), engraved or painted or both.

Shells were rarely found in the excavation—conus, glycymeris, olivella, and cut beads from large bivalve shellfish appear in the Pottery Mound collection but only in sparse quantities. The necklaces in the paintings often contain white beads, almost certainly shell, interspersed with red ones, probably coral; yet not one coral bead was recovered from the excavation. The muralists depicted shells so casually, however, that despite the lack of concrete evidence they must have been a much-used element of decoration in this Anasazi town.

The Mystery of the "Spanish Priest"

The dramatic painting of the three figures from layer 14 on the north wall of Kiva 2 (fig. 66) has been identified by several researchers as a Spanish priest held prisoner by two Indians—perhaps one of the

Spanish priests killed in the Pueblo rebellion of 1680. Indeed, the figure is patently non-Anasazi. The skull cap may have been an attempt to show a tonsured head or the small cap worn by Catholic churchmen. The garrote held by the man with the scalplock was a common Spanish method of execution which may have been borrowed by the Indians.

This particular painting was very well preserved and there is no doubt about the details, but the identification of this central figure as that of a European is open to considerable question. The principal Pottery Mound site did not, from all indications, extend into the historical period. The small ruin formerly located at the very edge of the Puerco cutbank may have extended into the sixteenth century, but even this is extremely doubtful, and in any event Kiva 2 is in the main body of the ruin and is associated with the second building period. Inasmuch as the painting is on the fourteenth plaster layer, it can be placed in about the middle of that period. This painting was probably made about the year A.D. 1400—long before the adventurous Spaniards arrived in the New Mexico area.

Furthermore, no mention of a pueblo at this site was made in any of the early Spanish documents. Such an omission would have been most unusual, since the Spanish conquistadores and the priests accompanying them were very meticulous in recording all they found. Accounts and locations of Anasazi towns were prominent and detailed in their journals—records which later became the basis of the notorious encomienda and repartamiento systems by which the Spanish enslaved the Indians and took their lands.

When Coronado came to New Mexico in 1540, he followed an already established route up the Sonora River and across the present Arizona border near the site of the present town of Clifton, Arizona. He then marched northeast across the Little Colorado and Gila rivers, stopping at the Zuni pueblo of Hawiku. Moving eastward to the Rio Grande, Coronado may or may not have taken his small army across the Puerco Valley in the vicinity of Pottery Mound. Even if he accidentally missed this site, the two expeditions which followed him, led by Chamuscado and Espejo, almost certainly could not have missed it were the pueblo still inhabited. Both Chamuscado and Espejo described in detail the occupied pueblos of the Piro people and the Tiguas, which are contiguous to Pottery Mound. Coronado did not mention the Tigua pueblo of Isleta, indicating that he may have entered the Rio Grande Valley farther to the north. Isleta, however, was duly recorded by later Spanish explorers, and a mission was established there in 1629. If Pottery Mound had been occupied at that time, a mission would certainly have been established there also. Even if only a remnant population had existed then at Pottery Mound, the Spaniards would certainly have recorded that fact.

The first actual historical account of this entire area was recorded by Don Juan de Oñate, who entered the Rio Grande at El Paso del Norte and, on April 20, 1598, claimed all of New Mexico in the name of his king, Felipe III of Spain. Oñate had in his entourage

Fig. 66. The mysterious figure in the center is flanked by two non-Anasazi Indians. These figures are discussed in detail on pages 78 and 88-93. (KIVA 2, LAYER 14, NORTH WALL)

Color photograph of the "Spanish priest" group as it appeared on the kiva wall. The paintings immediately began to lose brilliance when exposed to sunlight and air. As a result, the colors in this photograph are muted; compare with the artist's drawing in figure 66.

Mexican Indians and priests, *the first opportunity that most Anasazi pueblos would have had to see a Spanish priest.* Oñate served as governor of the "Kingdom of New Mexico" from 1598 until 1608, and spent most of that time exploring the country in search of the ever-elusive mineral wealth which had first lured the Spaniards there. His first capital, San Gabriel, was abandoned by deserting colonists in 1605, but the reluctant Spaniards were forced to return by the authorities in New Spain. All these comings and goings were duly and painstakingly recorded, but in none of these records was mention made of a pueblo at the site of Pottery Mound.

During the early days of the colonial period, the friars were busy converting the Anasazi to Catholicism and building missions at the occupied centers. All these missions have left records of their founding. The relationship between the Anasazi and the Franciscan friars was generally a peaceful one; it was often the friars who took the part of the Indians in dealings with their cruel masters, the Spanish civil and military authorities, who dealt so harshly with the Indian population.

In this same period Santa Fe was founded and named as a royal villa. Imposing mission churches were built at the Piro and Tigua pueblos east of the Rio Grande. A church and a monastery called Nuestra Señora de Socorro were built in 1626 at the site which is now Socorro, New Mexico, close to the area in question. The mission churches of San Luis Obispo at

Sevilleta, near the small town of the same name; Alamillo, a few miles farther north; and San Pascual, near the present town of San Antonio de Senecu, were all built in this period.

All these sites and missions are only a short distance from Pottery Mound. Farther to the west, the pueblo of Acoma at first resisted the Spaniards but later submitted to them, and a mission church was built there. (Laguna, of course, was not in existence in this early colonial period.) The routes of Spanish soldiers and Franciscan friars moving to and fro among the Anasazi towns of the Rio Grande Valley, Acoma, and the Zuni pueblos to the west would have taken them necessarily across the area of Pottery Mound. Indeed, in the early colonial period the Puerco Valley was used as a regular route of travel. If Spanish soldiers actually did ride over the site of Pottery Mound, the painting in question already lay buried deep beneath the hooves of their horses, and the pueblo was a ruin of rubble.

Supporting the fact that Pottery Mound predated the Spanish period is the lack in all of the murals of any suggestion of the Comanche or Apache. The muralists at this site did depict Indians of different tribes and could scarcely have missed the Apache, who were attacking Anasazi towns throughout the entire area during the Spanish occupation. Indeed, when the Pueblo Revolt against Spanish rule took place in 1680, the Apache had caused the abandonment of all Anasazi towns east of the Manzano Mountains. The Apache on several occasions killed Franciscan friars; and, once the Pueblo Revolt got underway, killings and mutilations of friars and other Spanish colonists were frequent.

The Spaniards were driven out of New Mexico by the Pueblo peoples, united in their hatred, and Spanish rule was kept out of the area for twelve years following the revolt—until the reconquest of 1692. During the revolt and the troubled times thereafter, the episode recorded on the wall of Kiva 2 might well have taken place. But the dating and the rest of the evidence do not support this theory.

It has also been suggested that the individual with the garrote around his neck may have been a Spanish fugitive from the colonies in Florida. Again because of the time element this would have been impossible; this painting was completed a century before the voyage of Columbus.

Birds and Feathers

The most common single element in the Pottery Mound frescoes is feathers, of various kinds and colors. Feathers appear in all aspects of Pueblo rituals in both prehispanic and modern times. They are used on masks, headdresses, staffs, altars, prayer sticks, tiponis, aspergilla, rattles, gourds, medicine-society standards, dance costumes, and many other ritualistic paraphernalia. (Note the feathered kilts in figures 25 and 26.)

With feathers naturally go the avifauna from which they are derived. That parrots and macaws were kept especially for their feathers is almost a certainty. Of the more than three hundred paintings or fragments of paintings showing birds, over two hun-

Fig. 67. *This figure with a feathered staff, blue body-paint, and a belt of animal skin carries a buffalo headdress, suggesting that he is an Indian from the Great Plains.* (KIVA 9, LAYER 3, WEST WALL)

dred contain either realistic or stylized parrots.

The use of the quetzal and the possible presence of live quetzals at Pottery Mound are much less certain. The crested birds in figures 14 (left of center) and 17 (far right) may depict quetzals, although they are the wrong color—red instead of green. The quetzal, of course, served often in a ceremonial capacity in Mesoamerica. Since Pottery Mound priests were familiar with the military macaw, which came from southern Mexico, it would seem logical that they also knew of the quetzal.

Following parrots and macaws in frequency are paintings of eagles. The bald eagle seems to be the favorite, probably because of its distinctive white and dark-brown or white and black colors. The bird with the jaguar in figure 47 is probably an eagle, and the stylization in figure 68 is probably also an eagle, although the colors are bizarre. Eagle wings, eagle claws, or both are often combined with human or animal figures. Figure 1 is an eagle dancer with feathered wings on the arms.

Ducks were present in three of the paintings. One example is the bird associated with the Anasazi to the far left in figure 14. The relationship of the duck to water makes it a natural inclusion in connection with rainmaking. The muralists of Pottery Mound generalized the duck paintings, i.e., the outlines are definitely those of ducks, but the species represented are difficult to determine.

Swallows appear several times, as in figure 14 (left-hand page, top center). In modern Pueblo usage swallows are also associated with rain, as "they live in

Fig. 68. *This elaborate, colorful bird is probably an eagle. The bird-like elements appearing on its body appear on several bird figures and on human dancers dressed as birds.* (KIVA 9, LAYER 3, WEST WALL)

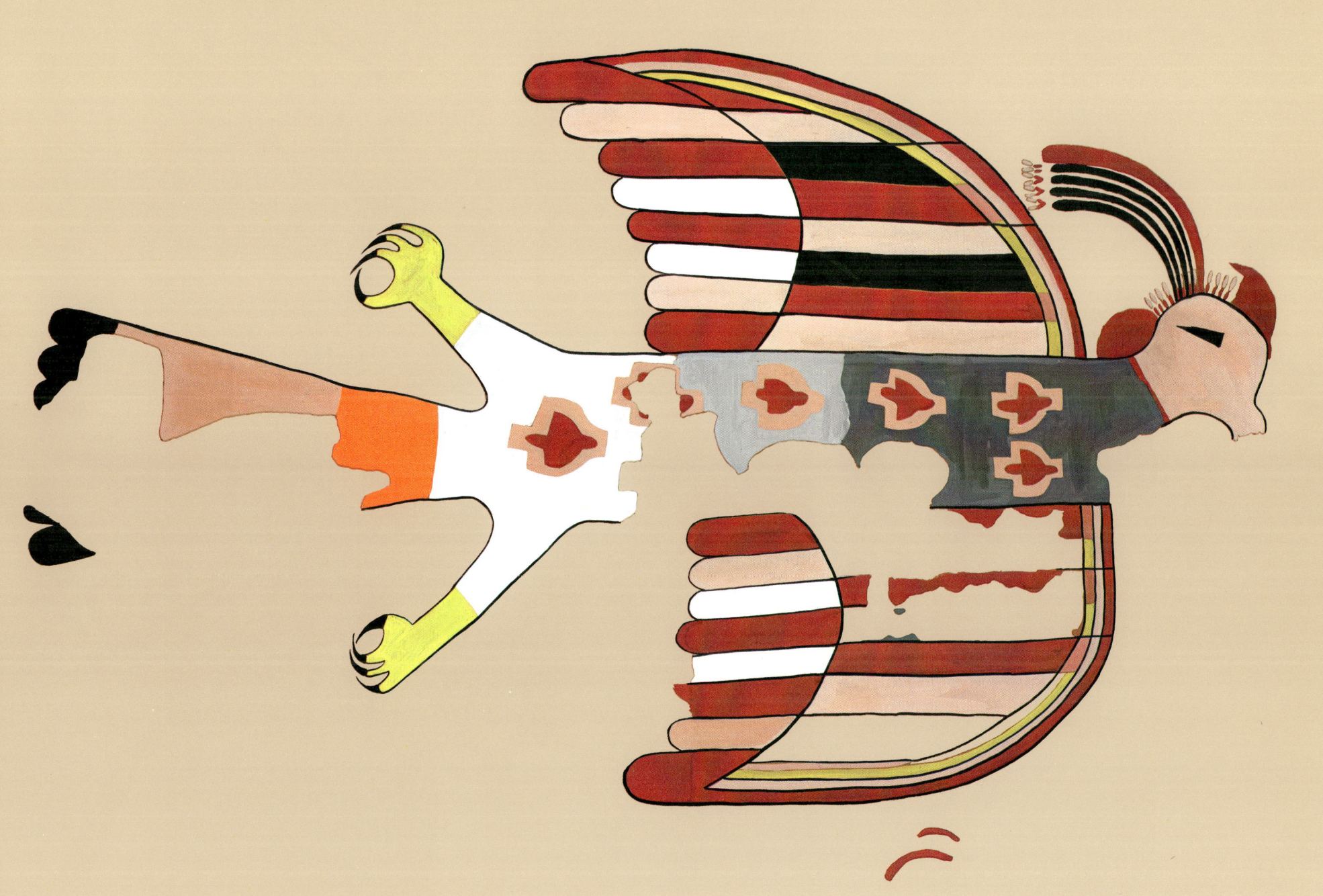

Fig. 69. *A zoomorphic combination of a bird and human legs. The outline of the bird suggests a swallow.* (KIVA 8, LAYER 1, WEST WALL)

wet places," in the words of an Acoma informant. Figure 69 is a swallow with human legs, probably a dancer dressed as a swallow.

Bird tracks appear many times, but it is difficult to determine the birds to which they belong. They may be those of the wild turkey, heron, or any other variety of bird having three large toes.

Birds which appear in various parts of the Pottery Mound murals may represent directions. Stevenson (1915, pp. 72, 89) reported that at Zuni various birds were indicative of directions: "North, long-tailed chat; west, long-crested jay; south, macaw; east, spurred towhee; zenith, purple martin or eagle; nadir, painted bunting."

The whooping crane is represented in figure 17. The bare neck sack is distended as it is when this large bird is engaged in the mating act.

The use of feathers, especially certain varieties, is primarily associated with rain and the universal Pueblo preoccupation with petitions to supernatural powers for rain. Eagle tail-feathers on Hopi costumes are "white cloud wings" (Stephen 1936). A Zuni kachina is fitted with owl feathers on his mask to "bring the rain" (Bunzel 1932). Feathers of various sorts are attached to prayer sticks and other paraphernalia used in ceremonies petitioning for rain.

Watson Smith (1952), in his excellent monograph on the mural decorations at Awatovi and Kawaika-a, has analyzed the ritualistic use of feathers as they appear in the paintings at those sites. There is little doubt that Pottery Mound usage parallels that in the Hopi area. In the Pottery Mound series, however, several thousands of feather representations occur, some of which differ from those at Awatovi or do not appear there at all.

Following the premise that Pottery Mound was associated with Acoma or other Keresan-speaking pueblos, a number of elderly Acoma informants were asked about the use of feathers. All replied that specific kinds of feathers were used in rainmaking ceremonies and for other purposes as well. They also said that in certain instances substitutions could be made if the feathers of a particular bird were not available. Dr. Matthew Stirling (1942), in his work on the Acoma origin myths, quotes an informant as saying that "nowadays just pretty feathers are used," but most other sources say flatly that the feathers of different birds served specific purposes. Apparently, among modern Pueblos, certain functionaries are orthodox in the use of particular feathers for particular ritualistic gear, and others are not so rigid. Perhaps, during the time in which the Pottery Mound frescoes were painted, supplies of feathers from a wide variety of wild birds were dependable and adequate, and orthodoxy in feather rituals was strictly followed.

Kenneth Chapman (1927), in studies of Pueblo pottery, has pointed out quite rightly that the elaborate use of feathers in rituals is not of extremely ancient origin. As a matter of fact, feathers were used copiously in Pueblo IV times, possibly in the Rio Grande area itself. It is even very probable that the elaborate use of feathers in rituals may have developed right there at Pottery Mound, since this was a sacred site of great significance. Also, the Pottery Mound pueblo, of all the Anasazi towns of Pueblo IV times, seems to have had the closest relationship with Mexico. Traffic in live birds, bird skins or feathers may have proceeded from Mexico to Pottery Mound and then to other Anasazi towns.

Feathers from the birds on the following list have been identified with fair certainty from the mural paintings at Pottery Mound. They appear in the order of frequency, beginning with the most common.

> Bald eagle (*Haliaeetus leucocephalus*)
> Raven or crow (*Corvus corax* or *Corvus brachyrhynchos*)
> Yellow-headed blackbird (*Xanthocephalus xanthocephalus*)
> Roadrunner (*Geococcyx californianus*)
> Yellow warbler (*Dendroica petechia*)
> Phainopepla (*Phainopepla nitens*)
> Wild turkey (*Meleagris gallopavo merriami*)
> Mallard duck (*Anas platyrhynchos*)
> Macaw (*Ara militaris* and *macao*)
> Quetzal (*Pharomachrus mocinno*)
> Parrot (*Rhynchopsitta pachyrhyncha*)
> Horned owl (*Bubo virginianus*)
> Yellow-breasted chat (*Icteria virens*)
> Magpie (*Pica pica*)
> Pileated (?) woodpecker (*Dryocopus pileatus*)
> Bluebird (*Sialia mexicana* or *Sialia currocoides*)
> Red-tailed hawk (*Buteo jamaicensis*)

This list comprises less than ten percent of all the feathers in the paintings. The remaining feathers are either too difficult or impossible to definitely identify. In some instances it would seem that the ancient muralists depicted a generalized feather. Perhaps, even in prehispanic times, substitution of one feather for another was allowable.

Fig. 70. Various elements are contained within a framing line. A thick-billed parrot pulls himself up by his beak on the corner of the frame. Color photograph of the original painting appears at right. (KIVA 7, LAYER 31, WEST WALL)

Fig. 71. Two human figures in unusual dress grasp an eagle in a scene representing the ceremonial capture of an eagle for its feathers. (KIVA 16, LAYER 3, WEST WALL)

The eagle tail-feather is used commonly, but its place at the very top of the frequency list for Pottery Mound is perhaps only because its white body and black tip are so easily identified in the paintings. The eagle tail-feather is commonly depicted by modern Pueblo artists and also often adorns dance costumes and other paraphernalia of modern Pueblos. Its use has been curtailed in recent years by federal laws protecting both the golden and bald eagles. The plains Indians, with whom the Anasazi at Pottery Mound were in contact, also regularly used eagle tail-feathers.

Often associated with rain, this feather has had other functions as well. It has been used at Laguna and Acoma in curing ceremonies to drive away evil (Parsons 1926). In the Hopi Snake Dance, as each dancer holds a serpent in his mouth his assistant uses eagle tail-feathers to stroke or "whip" the snake.

In ancient, as in modern times, Pueblos caught eagles in a ceremonial manner, by digging a pit and covering it with a lattice-work of branches upon which a live rabbit was tethered. Dressed in ceremonial costumes and with appropriate accompanying ritual to placate the spirit of the eagle, the eagle-catchers, usually two in number, waited in the pit until an eagle stooped to kill the rabbit and then grasped the bird by its feet. Figure 71 probably depicts the capturing of an eagle.

The feathers of the golden eagle are almost certainly depicted in the Pottery Mound frescoes, but because of their less distinctive appearance they cannot be absolutely identified. Some feathers of a yellowish or brownish color were undoubtedly meant to be those of the golden eagle. At present-day Acoma the down feathers of the golden eagle or wild turkey are frequently used to convey prayers. Indeed, down feathers from many varieties of birds are used to wing petitions and prayers to supernatural powers. Down feathers have a mystic ability to float, even in still air. An Acoma adviser recounts that the down feathers placed on prayer sticks or on the tips of evergreen branches "carry the prayer to those who are dead."

The feathers of the Merriam (wild) turkey are used widely among modern Pueblos; the Rio Grande Pueblos use them more often than any other variety. Modern makers of prayer plumes and other ritual gear insist on the feathers of wild turkeys, and seldom if ever use the feathers of domestic turkeys, which are of course descendants of the Mexican wild turkey. This is in sharp contrast to the very common use of chicken feathers—dyed red, green, and blue—to decorate kachinas or dance costumes.

Only a comparatively few turkey feathers could be identified in the Pottery Mound murals. Tail feathers of the Merriam turkey are banded at the tips and its wing feathers are barred; both are thus identifiable. Several of the black-and-white-barred or brown-and-white-barred feathers in the paintings are probably wild turkey. Breast feathers of the wild turkey can be identified by their generally square ends and sometimes by their triangular shapes.

All black feathers were identified more or less positively as those of the raven or crow. In modern Pueblo usage the raven is associated with death and with the bringing of rain, which the dead—dwelling in the sky—have the power to send. In the Hopi war dance, raven feathers are worn or carried to signify that the raven will feed upon the enemies slain by the dancing warriors (Stephen 1936). Hopi who have completed the burying of one of their dead are exorcised with raven feathers (Stephen 1936). The elaborately kilted dancer in figure 72 is holding what is probably a raven.

Yellow-and-black feathers are probably those of the yellow-headed blackbird, common in this area especially during migration. Yellow-and-black feathers or plain yellow ones are used for the Hopi flute ceremony. Yellow feathers from the yellow-headed blackbird or the yellow warbler appear on Acoma prayer sticks.

The roadrunner symbolizes speed, and its long tail-feathers are used as ritualistic whips and for prayer plumes. The roadrunner can be positively identified in at least three stylized bird depictions in the murals. Other instances are less certain.

The feathers of the drake mallard duck can be identified in a few instances. Green feathers may be from the head of the drake mallard or from the green quetzal. The curling feathers from the tail of the drake mallard are distinctive and recognizable. These curling feathers are favorites with modern Pueblos for prayer sticks and other uses. They also use the feathers of other varieties of wild duck.

Macaws and parrots have already been noted in the discussion of Mexican influences. Paintings of entire birds are very common in the Pottery Mound frescoes—the hooked beak and colored plumage are

Fig. 72. The bird carried by this dancer is probably a raven. The dancer's dress features a bandoleer, arm decorations, ankle bands, and an especially elaborate kilt which was applied with thick paint and then incised. (KIVA 1, LAYER 1, EAST WALL)

distinctive, but only a very few of the single feathers can be definitely identified as macaw or parrot. Macaw and parrot feathers may be red, green, blue, yellow, or a combination of these colors. Modern Pueblos value parrot feathers above all others and use them whenever they are available.

Several of the black-and-brown-barred feathers of the great horned owl can be pointed out with fair certainty. Owl feathers, especially those of the horned owl, are much used among modern Pueblos. The owl is associated with rain, and also with death.

The distinctive black-and-white feathers of the magpie can be located in a few instances, although some of the black-and-white feathers may be confused with those of the bald eagle. Feathers of the magpie are also used by modern Pueblos.

Wholly red feathers or red-and-black feathers probably are those of the woodpecker, such as the one in figure 14 (far left). Modern Pueblos use feathers from all species of woodpecker. The males of several of these species sport red-and-black feathers and white feathers with black crossbars.

Blue-colored feathers appear in the Pottery Mound murals and are presumably those of the western or the mountain bluebird. Blue feathers could also come from the blue grosbeak, jay, or kingfisher. Acoma informants say these blue feathers represent the bluebird, because "that is the rain bird."

Reddish or orange feathers with black barring are from the tail of the red-tailed hawk (the headdress in figure 73), or they may be from the sparrow hawk. The fletching feathers of arrows in the quivers of the warriors and animals in the council of the mountain lions in Kiva 6 (title page) appear to be those of the red-tailed hawk.

In figure 73 the ancient muralists obviously intended to depict certain kinds of feathers, and they painted outlines, designs, and colors to convey particular ideas. Many of these identifications must await further study and the attention of ornithologists of different backgrounds.

Two members of the Audubon Society of Albuquerque, New Mexico, and members of the faculty of the University of New Mexico assisted with the identifications of the various birds and feathers. Although they did not in every case agree, a consensus was reached, and the above material is the result of their observations.

Prayer Sticks and Tiponis

Pahos, or prayer sticks, are made and used in all modern Pueblo villages. The general form is a stick, usually painted, to which one or more feathers are attached. Some pahos may be pointed at one end, so they can be thrust into the ground (figs. 7, 60). Others have a tip that is bent over and tied to the shaft in the manner of a lacrosse stick. Still others have small cylinders, discs, or a potsherd in the form of a disc bound to the top with string. Modern pahos occur in a bewildering variety of forms. It is safe to say that no Pueblo ritual could be carried on without pahos. The proliferation of pahos apparently occurred in Pueblo IV at the time that feather usage increased; the two go together.

Fig. 73. Headdress made of eagle feathers from which protrude extensions of roadrunner (?) and hawk (?) feathers. (KIVA 8, LAYER 5, SW CORNER

Fig. 74. *Anasazi maiden (hairdo) with feather headdress carries a pot in one hand and an aspergill in the other. In rainmaking ceremonies the aspergill was dipped into the water pot and then sprinkled to simulate rain.* (KIVA 8, LAYER 1, WEST WALL)

Pahos can be identified in at least twenty-three of the Pottery Mound murals and less certainly in many of the fragments recovered from other paintings. Many of the dancing figures hold in their hands feathers or bunches of feathers which are probably pahos (fig. 2). Tufts of feathers occurring on the ground line in some paintings are apparently pahos stuck into the ground.

The Corn Mother, or *tiponi*, depicted often in the Pottery Mound paintings (fig. 5), is another sacred object used extensively among all modern Pueblo villages. The tiponi is made of a perfect ear of corn with various long feathers attached to it at one end with wrapped string. The string is coiled around the ear so that the corn itself is not actually visible. In some instances a base is formed with string so that the tiponi can be set upright on the ground (title page). An Acoma informant reports that Acoma tiponi makers always use parrot feathers if they can get them. In other pueblos turkey, magpie, woodpecker, and other bird feathers are used.

Several bundles of feathers which are probably tiponis appear throughout the Pottery Mound frescoes, an assumption based on the fact that the Pueblos believe the Corn Mother is the originator of all life. During medicine-society rituals the chief of that society carries a tiponi in his hand, and the chief of the underworld carries a tiponi. This sacred corn ear with the fetish is thus used to identify a priest.

Other feather bundles appear in the murals; these may be complex prayer-stick bundles, or aspergilla. Modern Pueblos use a bundle of long feathers—

Fig. 75. The second figure on this wall is a male with an elaborate feather headdress. He, too, carries an aspergill and a pot, from which water is splashing. Color photograph of the original appears above. (KIVA 8, LAYER 1, WEST WALL)

usually bald-eagle tail-feathers, turkey wing-feathers, or raven feathers—to sprinkle water on dancers or their paraphernalia. This may be a modern Pueblo adaptation of the Roman Catholic use of aspergilla; however, some of the Pottery Mound paintings containing a bundle of feathers held in hand suggest that this general function may have been in use in prehistoric times. Aspergilla at present are used to "bless" various participants or paraphernalia to make rain, to exorcise, and to indicate direction. The woman and the man in figures 74 and 75 seem to be using a bundle of feathers in an attempt to bring rain.

Fig. 76. In this exquisite painting a stylized figure in an elaborate costume dances with a parrot in one hand and feathers in the other. She is flanked (left) by a "bird man" and (right) by a "squash maiden," a "bear man," a ghost figure descending from above, and another bird man. (KIVA 2, LAYER 2, SOUTH WALL)

Mammals

Animals are almost as important in Pueblo ritual as birds and feathers. A number of Pueblo myths deal with animals, and several are regarded as totemic or clan ancestors. Many Pueblo stories tell how certain animals acquired characteristics such as speed, hunting ability, craftiness, or keen eyesight.

Much ritual usage dictates that certain animal skins or parts thereof must be worn with a particular dance costume. Thus, coyote skins are worn by the hunters in hunting dances because "the coyote hunts so well." Wolf skins are used, if they can be acquired, for the same reason. Gray-fox skins are worn in the back of the belt for the kachina-dance costume. Hunting practices involve rituals which must be observed in treating game animals. Thus, when a Pueblo hunter has killed a deer, and after the appropriate chant, he cleans the carcass in a prescribed manner. He removes the eyes of the animal and takes them back to the mountains "so the deer cannot see the hunter when he hunts again."

MOUNTAIN LION. The puma, cougar, or mountain lion is one of the most spectacular animals in the Southwest, and it is prominent in Pueblo and Anasazi lore. No fewer than nineteen depictions of the mountain lion appear in the Pottery Mound frescoes. Other manifestations of the cougar are in a stylized form (fig. 78) and in the form of arrow quivers apparently made of a lion skin complete with long tail (fig. 49, right of center). Most of the lions in the Pottery Mound series are in a crouching position, and often a small lion appears underneath the female or between the front

107

Fig. 78. A feather-edged shield covers the body of a stylized mountain lion. (KIVA 7, LAYER 11, WEST WALL)

paws (fig. 77). In the mountain-lion council in Kiva 6 (title page), the lions are shown in the same aspect as their fellow human councilors—sitting up and carrying quivers of arrows. It is interesting that the claws, one of the major features of the cougar, are carefully and prominently displayed and distended, even though this occasionally produces an unnatural perspective. The black-tipped tail, upright ears, and side whiskers are very well done in some of the paintings, evidence that the Pottery Mound muralists were familiar with this animal. Some depictions of the cougar are, in contrast, quite stiff and formal.

The Acoma observers at the site were very excited about the paintings of mountain lions at Pottery Mound, especially Mr. Chino, head of the war society at Acoma. The cougar is associated with the war societies in Keresan pueblos and at Jemez, but at Zuni the cougar is a symbol of the hunting society.

WOLF. The wolf is a rare Pottery Mound depiction, but the animal in figure 79 is without doubt such an animal. The ancient muralist was so impressed by the tracks of the wolf that he displayed the wolf's body quite accurately from the side view and then tipped the feet up to show its tracks.

Fig. 77. A mountain lion, on which a rattlesnake is superimposed, is associated with an unidentified animal to the right and above. A small mountain lion appears between its paws, and a sprig of evergreen appears below the body. (KIVA 16, LAYER 4, WEST WALL)

Fig. 79. An animal, probably a wolf, carries a quiver made of mountain-lion skin. A human figure with face-paint appears at right. (KIVA 16, LAYER 4, EAST WALL)

Now extinct in the Southwest, the wolf must have been common in Pottery Mound times. Modern Pueblos associate the wolf with hunting and the chase; it also symbolizes swiftness. The Acoma avow that the wearing of a wolf skin will make a runner tireless.

JAGUAR. The northern range of the jaguar rarely extends beyond the present United States-Mexico boundary. The Anasazi of Pottery Mound must have been familiar with this animal in the area of the lower Rio Grande or farther south into Old Mexico.

The jaguar in figure 47, from Kiva 6 (on the same layer as the mountain-lion council), is well drawn and easily recognized. The eagle between the paws of the jaguar is a possible tie-in with the Mexican eagle-jaguar cult. An especially fine painting of a jaguar was found in Kiva 17, recently under excavation. This painting depicts all four legs in a very natural manner. Unfortunately, the head of this particular jaguar was destroyed by careless pothunters previous to excavation.

Keresan-speaking and other modern Pueblos are

vaguely familiar with the jaguar, but apparently refer to it as a *rohona*. Dr. Leslie White (1943) has investigated the rohona and found that it was probably a jaguar remembered dimly from ancient times. Other Pueblos have identified the rohona as the mountain lion, coyote, weasel, lynx, etc., but Dr. White remains convinced that the rohona was a jaguar and was associated with the war society.

COYOTE. Mention of the coyote is frequent in Pueblo folklore, yet it is difficult to identify in the Pottery Mound paintings. The animal in figure 80 is probably a coyote, but many of the animals pictured at Pottery Mound are rather nondescript and could be wolf, coyote, dog, fox, or the mysterious rohona.

SKUNK. The design in the medallion in figure 56 is thought to be a skunk because of its bushy tail and the stripes on its back. The head, however, could be that of a bear, badger, or any other animal. Several other figures in the murals suggest the skunk, but these identifications are not even as clear as the one in the medallion. Skunk skins are used in a number of Pueblo costumes although not as often as those of other animals. Also, the skunk is not of major importance in Anasazi lore.

BEAR. Several animals in the Pottery Mound series, such as the bright blue one in figure 33, are apparently bears—either grizzlies or black bears. None seems to be as well drawn as the figures of the cougar, jaguar, wolf, and some other animal species.

The bear is very powerful medicine in modern Pueblo rituals. At Zuni the bear is an animal of great strength associated with war; and bear fetishes are

Fig. 80. A dog-like animal, probably a coyote.
(KIVA 7, LAYER 21, SOUTH WALL)

common, as they were in ancient times. Three bear fetishes were found at Pottery Mound. At Acoma bears are associated with the hunting and fire societies (Stirling 1942). Among the eastern Pueblos the bear is greatly feared. Bear meat is eaten and bear skins or bear paws are worn only with the accompaniment of elaborate ritual and at considerable peril to the user.

FOX. Like the wolf and the dog, the fox is difficult to identify in this series. The fox is prominent in Pueblo usage, and fox skins are part of the standard kachina costume.

Fig. 81. This pronghorn antelope wears a necklace, indicating that it is an effigy animal used in dances and ceremonies and not a live animal. (KIVA 2, LAYER 16, WEST WALL)

112

Fig. 82. Lizard-like animal, probably a Gila monster. (KIVA 2, LAYER 11 OR 12, SOUTH WALL)

ANTELOPE. Antelope are shown in two ways in the Pottery Mound murals: One is the live animal; the other is a representation using an antelope skin (or possibly the head or body) mounted on a framework for use in a hunting dance. An example of the latter is figure 81, which has bead strands on its neck. The inhabitants of Pottery Mound were very familiar with the antelope. Early U.S. Army documents report large herds of antelope in the Puerco Valley in the middle of the nineteenth century.

Fully-clothed antelope dancers are regularly featured in the hunting dances of modern Pueblos. An Acoma informant reports that the antelope skin, with the head and horns erect on a stick, is often carried as concealment for the hunter as he approaches this wary animal.

DEER. Although deer bones were the most common mammal remains in the refuse at Pottery Mound, none of the animals in the paintings can definitely be identified as a deer. Some of the headdresses, such as those in figure 17, contain what may be deer antlers. Figure 48 may be a deer, despite claws and long tail.

Snakes and Reptiles

Rattlesnakes appear often in the Pottery Mound frescoes. Some apparently live reptiles are represented (fig. 20), and snakeskins also appear (fig. 49). Such skins are used in modern Pueblo rituals in connection with rain and rainmaking. The deadly aspect of the rattlesnake undoubtedly intrigues present-day Pueblos, as it did their Anasazi ancestors.

The horned and feathered serpent, which appears six times in the Pottery Mound murals, has been

Fig. 83. A human figure, carrying feathers and other elements, wears a mask with the horn and plumes of the feathered serpent.
(KIVA 7, LAYER 21, WEST WALL)

Fig. 84. *Spotted dragonflies hover near a corn plant.*
(KIVA 7, LAYER 26?, NE CORNER)

Fig. 85. *A humanized dragonfly. The scalloped red lines may represent dragonfly eggs.* (KIVA 7, LAYER 4, SE SECTION)

referred to as a Mesoamerican motif. Quetzalcoatl, as the Mexicans know this serpent god, is often mentioned in Mexican religions and folklore. Its appearance at Pottery Mound coincides with other borrowings from Mexico.

The snake-like creature in figure 42 may or may not be a part of the Quetzalcoatl legend. This serpent or reptile is apparently devouring a human.

The reptile in figure 82 may be a Gila monster or a salamander. Its brilliant color would seem to set it apart as some sort of mythological monster.

Insects

The dragonfly is associated with water, and thus rain, in both modern and ancient usage. It appears more often in the Pottery Mound series than any other insect—in over thirty paintings, usually with a single body having one to three sets of wings. Sometimes they are spotted or dotted (fig. 84), and occasionally they appear as very simple crosses (fig. 45). Dragonfly designs also appear in several of the large abstract panels, and dragonflies were also carved into stone floor slabs in two of the kivas. Figure 85 is the "dragonfly man," according to Acoma informants.

The mosquito, like the dragonfly, is associated with water and rain. The proboscis of the mosquito is prominent in the zoomorphic figures of the "mosquito men" in figures 45 and 86.

The human-headed insect figures appearing in figure 8 may be grasshoppers or cicadas. An Acoma informant said this painting was a creation scene, but he would give no further information.

Fig. 86. A "mosquito man," with feather headdress and gossamer wings, wears short trousers instead of the usual kilt. Color photograph of the original appears at left. (KIVA 7, LAYER 10, SOUTH WALL)

Fig. 87. *Composite of two bodies in human form representing, according to the Acoma, two aspects of mankind.* (KIVA 8, LAYER 6, SOUTH WALL)

Zoomorphs

In many of the paintings human, animal, and bird features are combined into one form (figs. 1, 2, 31, 69, 88). The single painting in figure 76 contains several of these composite figures, or *zoomorphs*. In addition to the human-headed insects in figure 8, human body parts are combined with those of the bear, eagle, parrot, antelope, wolf, and other animals less easily identified. Future studies will undoubtedly correlate these strange creatures with origin myths, legends, and other Anasazi folklore.

Fig. 88. Composite animal, bird, and human figure carrying a branch. Six "ribbons" appear on the body; these decorations appear on many figures—both animal and human—in the murals. (KIVA 9, LAYER 3, SOUTH WALL)

Spirit Figures

Many of the mural paintings depict spirits. Some of these are human in form but appear in odd combinations (figs. 58, 87). Figure 89 is of human form—apparently a ghost descending from the sky. Others in the frescoes are only vaguely human or animal—figure 90 contains both a vague, ghostly human shape (left) and a bizarre animal shape (right). Figure 11 is a composite of two human shapes.

These ghostly figures are in keeping with the beliefs of the kachina cult of the Pueblos, in which the spirits of humans, animals, birds, plants, and even nonliving things such as rivers and mountains are received by the kachina ceremonial dancers wearing corresponding masks (Bahti 1970). The Pueblos are especially respectful of the spirits of dead ancestors. To prevent the ghosts of the dead from returning unexpectedly, i.e., when they are not expressly called upon, prayer sticks are offered to the spirits of the deceased. The kachina masks in figures 9 and 10 are probably those of such spirits. The trailing spirals of beads may indicate descent from the clouds.

Fig. 89. A ghost-like human figure descends from the sky. (KIVA 8, LAYER 3, SOUTH WALL)

Fig. 90. These two esoteric figures probably represent the spirits of a dead human and an animal. (KIVA 2, LAYER 2, NORTH WALL)

Textiles

One of the richest treasures to be derived from the Pottery Mound murals is the wide array of textiles appearing in them. It is known that prehispanic Pueblos regularly wove clothing and blankets; in fact, it was from the Anasazi that the Navajo learned their weaving art. Little, however, is known of early Anasazi textiles (Kent 1957), and the earliest Navajo blanket barely extends back to the beginning of the nineteenth century. Most modern Pueblos have given up weaving altogether, with the exception of the Hopi.

Over a thousand textiles and textile designs appear in the Pottery Mound series. All these textiles were presumably made of native cotton, as wool and other animal fibers were unobtainable prior to the coming of the Spaniards.

Fig. 91. *A female figure, apparently pregnant, with face-paint and a headdress simulating the new moon.* (KIVA 2, LAYER 4, EAST WALL)

Fig. 92. *This example of the black-and-white kilt common in the paintings has some unusual elements and finely detailed tassels.* (KIVA 1, LAYER 1, WEST WALL)

Fig. 93. Three kilted figures dance with staffs. The central figure has an especially elaborate kilt and arm designations. (KIVA 1, LAYER 1, SOUTH WALL)

A constantly reappearing garment in the Pottery Mound series is the kilt, or short skirt, worn by both men and women (figs. 16, 75, 91). This kilt is decorated with a wide variety of designs, usually a series of white dots and lines against a dark background, in what is described by an Acoma informant as the "corn kernel" design. The kilt was gathered at the waist by a sash with tassels, some very elaborate, with multiple knots. These sashes often have smaller tassels hanging from them (title page). The kilts themselves are often extremely elaborate, such as those in figures 64, 65, and 72, and the one containing two stylized parrot designs worn in figure 93 (center). The kilt in figure 92 is an unusual variation of the black-and-white design and sports a sash with tassels exaggeratedly defined. The curious kilt worn by the man in figure 49 (far right) has vertical stripes and is secured with a snake-skin sash.

The usual women's garment was the *manta*, worn over one shoulder leaving the other shoulder bare, and was of a dark background decorated with white (figs. 45, 74, 99, 100). A similar one-piece gar-

121

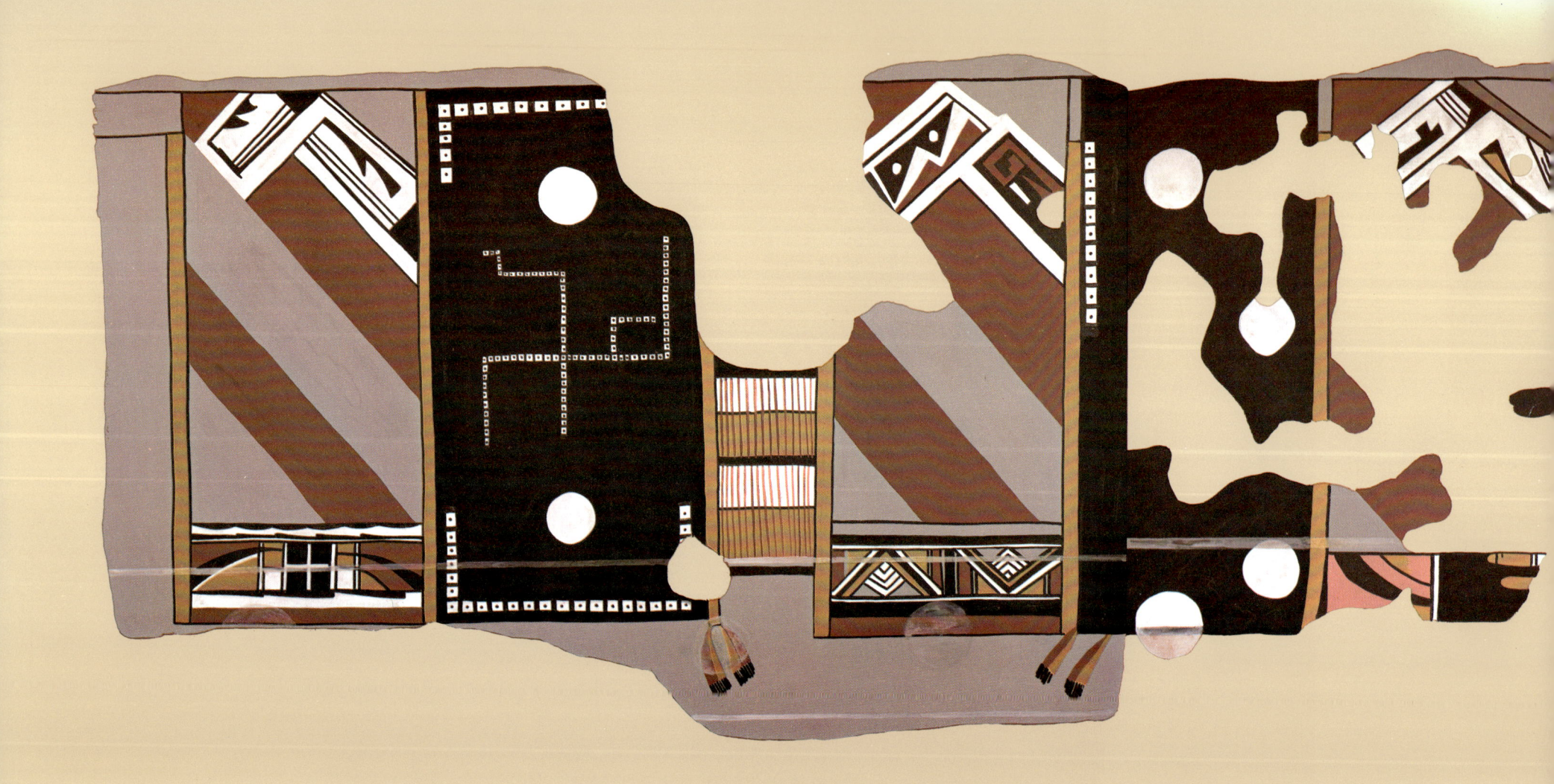

Fig. 94. Blankets with varying designs appear as if hanging from a rack. The motif of the hanging blankets extended all the way

ment was worn by Pueblo women as late as a few decades ago, and is now often used as a dance costume. Another women's costume, such as that in figure 76, has sleeves and an overblouse colorfully and elaborately decorated. In this particular figure, that of a dancer with an exquisite parrot in one hand and an aspergill in the other, the garment is decorated with stylized parrots. Still another unusual garment is the decorated blouse which starts under the arms, worn by the dancers in figures 38 and 62.

Several Anasazi, such as the ones engaged in rituals in figures 30 and 71, are dressed in special

around the four walls of Kiva 16. (KIVA 16, LAYER 11, WEST AND NORTH WALLS)

shirts. These very different designs undoubtedly have significance in these particular ceremonies.

From a general survey of the frescoes, it would appear that the black-and-white cotton garments of both men and women were their everyday attire, and that the more elaborate variations, short trousers, and striped skirts were ritual costumes for special ceremonies.

Several of the paintings, such as figures 94-96, are blankets. They are especially significant as examples of the weaving and design which the Navajo copied. Blankets in the Pottery Mound series reveal

Fig. 95. *A simple fret design, probably representing a textile.* (KIVA 10, LAYER 10, WEST WALL)

designs and shapes over three centuries older than any other known examples. In figure 17 (right, center), the blankets appear to be hanging on a rack or bar attached to the roof of the kiva. This is another example of a kiva painting displaying ritualistic gear as it was stored in the kiva.

The designs on the blankets vary widely but are noticeably different from those of clothing. Very early Navajo blankets (fig. 96) faintly resemble some of the Pottery Mound designs, and certainly this is no accident.

It is difficult to tell from the paintings just what weaving techniques were employed. A survey of the designs would seem to indicate that the Pottery Mound weavers certainly knew and used several methods. The kilt worn by the dancer in figure 72 was probably done in embroidery. This particular painting was done with very heavy paint in several layers

Fig. 96. *This blanket containing kiva-step and fret designs is an example of the kind of weaving copied by the Navajo when they first arrived in the Southwest.* (KIVA 12, LAYER 25, NORTH WALL)

Fig. 97. *This feather-edged shield is of a design similar to those which appear in Mexico.* (KIVA 7, LAYER 6, SOUTH WALL)

and also was incised, as though the ancient muralist had tried to depict the texture of the embroidery. Because of their close contact with Mexico, it is reasonable to assume that the Pottery Mound weavers were familiar with Mexican techniques.

The man at the far right in figure 49 wears a hat which appears distinct from the elaborate headdresses worn by other Anasazi. Four paintings in the series contain figures wearing hats.

Netting, such as that shown in figure 98, appears in several of the paintings. Pottery Mound workers apparently used these net bags for carrying loads. Netted gourds also appear, as the one held by the man second from left in figure 14.

Baskets

Basketry is a long-standing Anasazi tradition. Baskets, or basket fragments, have been recovered in a number of excavations. They all reveal basket-making techniques of manufacture but seldom retain decorations or color. Because of this lack, the paintings of the Pottery Mound series are especially valuable as records of prehistoric basketry.

The baskets carried by the maidens in figures 99 and 100 are examples of the twenty-odd representations of baskets. In some of the other paintings, it is difficult to tell whether baskets or pottery bowls were intended.

Carrying-baskets appear in three of the paintings (fig. 98). A few specimens of Anasazi carrying-baskets have been recovered from dry caves in the Southwest (Stephen 1936); they are similar to those in the Pottery Mound murals.

Fig. 98. *A woman carries a burden basket. Netting is used to contain the objects at the bottom of the basket, and a gourd appears on a shelf above. A parrot rides or is tethered to the edge; live parrots were undoubtedly transported in this manner from Mexico into Anasazi territory.* (KIVA 7, LAYER 14, SW CORNER)

Figs. 99-100. Anasazi maidens (hairdos) carry baskets and another object, perhaps a rattle. Cornstalks appear in this frieze. As in many other instances at Pottery

Mound, this motif extended all the way around the kiva in the same layer.
(KIVA 16, LAYER 1, EAST WALL)

Fig. 101. *A warrior carrying a spear and a shield with an elaborate mask, similar to a Mexican death mask, painted upon it. The shield is rimmed with turkey feathers.* (KIVA 9, LAYER 12, WEST WALL)

Shields

Although warfare among the Pueblos became virtually obsolete after early Spanish times, much ritual and paraphernalia derived from war practices persist through modern times. The war chiefs still enjoy great respect among Pueblos, and war societies still perform critical rituals.

At least one of the Pottery Mound kivas probably belonged to the war society, but it is difficult to ascertain which one it was. Paintings of warriors appeared in several of the kivas and in various layers.

Typical are the shield-bearers in figures 28 and 101-104. It is assumed that if the figures carry weapons and shields they are warriors. Figures carrying bows and other weapons, but not shields, could be hunters and/or warriors. A typical feather-edged shield with a central motif appears in figure 97.

Shields in several of the paintings appear as if hanging on a wall. Feather-edged shields and the designs on the shields are Mexican in character. The warrior to the far right in figure 103 is carrying a shield of leather without feather edging. It is interesting that warriors in figure 102 carry atlatls as well as bows and arrows.

Fig. 102. These shield-bearers carrying feather-edged shields, bows and arrows, and atlatls were on the west wall of a frieze extending around Kiva 2 on the same layer. Figures 103 and 104 on the following pages make this frieze nearly complete. (KIVA 2, LAYER 3, WEST WALL)

Figs. 103-104. The shield-bearer motif is continued (refer to fig. 102) on the north, east, and south walls of Kiva 2. The right-hand shield in figure 103 is

132

apparently made of leather. Many of the shield motifs are similar to Mexican designs. (KIVA 2, LAYER 3)

133

Fig. 105. Two rattlesnakes with "soul faces" and feather ruffs. These may represent spirits of the dead to whom the Anasazi appealed for rain and other benefits. (KIVA 8, LAYER 7, EAST WALL)

Stars

A constantly recurring motif at Pottery Mound is the four-pointed star with an inner circle containing a human face. Figures 106 and 107 are entire designs made up of these "soul faces," as described by the Acoma informants. Stars with faces also appear in other designs, such as that of the feathered serpent (fig. 34) and in conjunction with the rattlesnake (fig. 105). These have feather-plume headdresses and may be connected with the feathered-serpent motif. Multipointed stars appear in the design in figure 35.

Rainbows

Rainbows in various forms are prominent in Pueblo and Anasazi usage. Not only is this celestial phenomenon a very striking sight, especially in an arid country such as the Southwest, but the rainbow is vivid proof of a successful rain. Logically the rainbow should consist of an arcuate form with parallel bands of color of the spectrum ranging from violet to red. However, in Pueblo usage (and in Navajo sandpaintings), the colors do not follow the sequence of the spectrum and are not always arcuate.

In the Pottery Mound paintings parallel bands of color, presumably rainbows, occur in at least twelve combinations of color. Rainbow bands are commonly used as framing lines. Figures such as the "rainbow man" in figure 14 have rainbow bands on their backs to associate them with rain or rainmaking.

Figs. 106-107. These stars with human faces were identified by the Acoma as "soul faces." Some are upside down; others have feather ruffs or similar decorations. (KIVA 6, LAYER 1, WEST WALL)

Clouds and Lightning

Cloud symbols are common in Pueblo iconography and are found in a number of standard forms. Symbolic and geometric cloud representations occur in most of the design panels. The white clouds outlined in black in figure 8 are semi-realistic, symbolic piled-up rain clouds, according to Pueblo usage. Geometric figures, in which the sides are formed by a series of steps, usually represent clouds. This cloud pattern is usually, but not always, in the form of a cloud pyramid (fig. 37). When it is in the form of a half-pyramid, with one side straight and the other side stepped, it is known by modern Pueblos as a "kiva-step" design. Symbolic cloud representations of all these varieties appear frequently in the Pottery Mound series and are also common on pottery from the site. Cloud patterns also appear on the basketry and pottery in the paintings.

Lightning, with its obvious connection with rain, is a pattern recurring frequently on the altars, tablitas, and other ceremonial gear of modern Pueblos. In contrast to its frequent appearance in modern Pueblo iconography, lightning appears fairly infrequently in Pottery Mound frescoes. It is usually represented by zigzag lines or by a series of match-like sticks arranged in a zigzag pattern with ends overlapping (figs. 12, 45, 61, 108, 109). Modern Pueblo art and sandpaintings employ a motif similar to that in figure 109—lightning bolts emanating from a cloud mass.

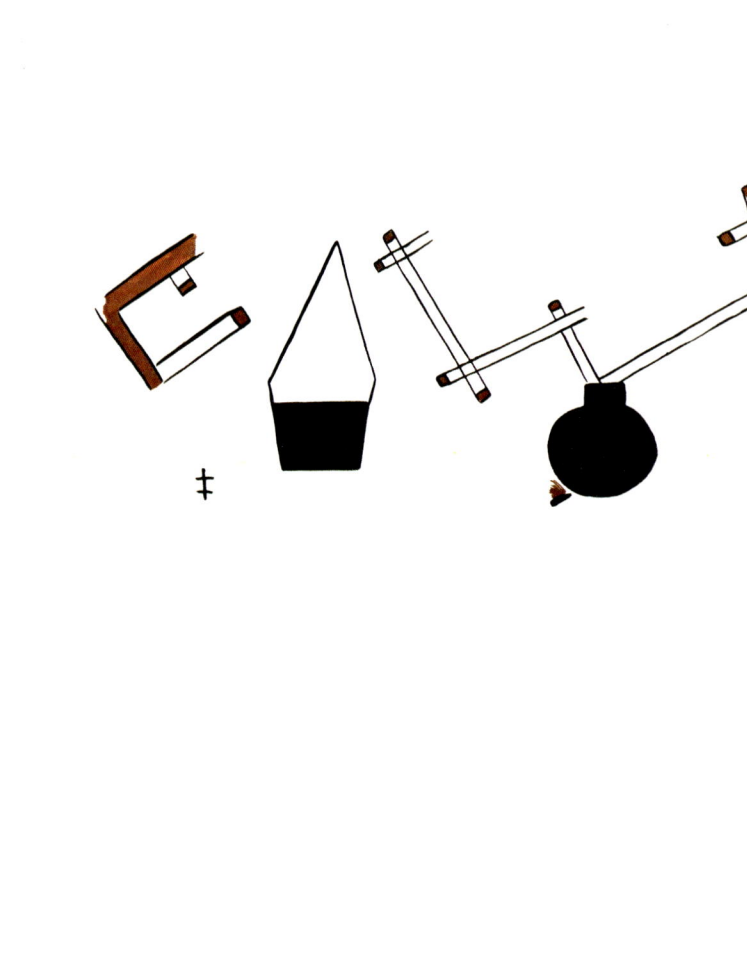

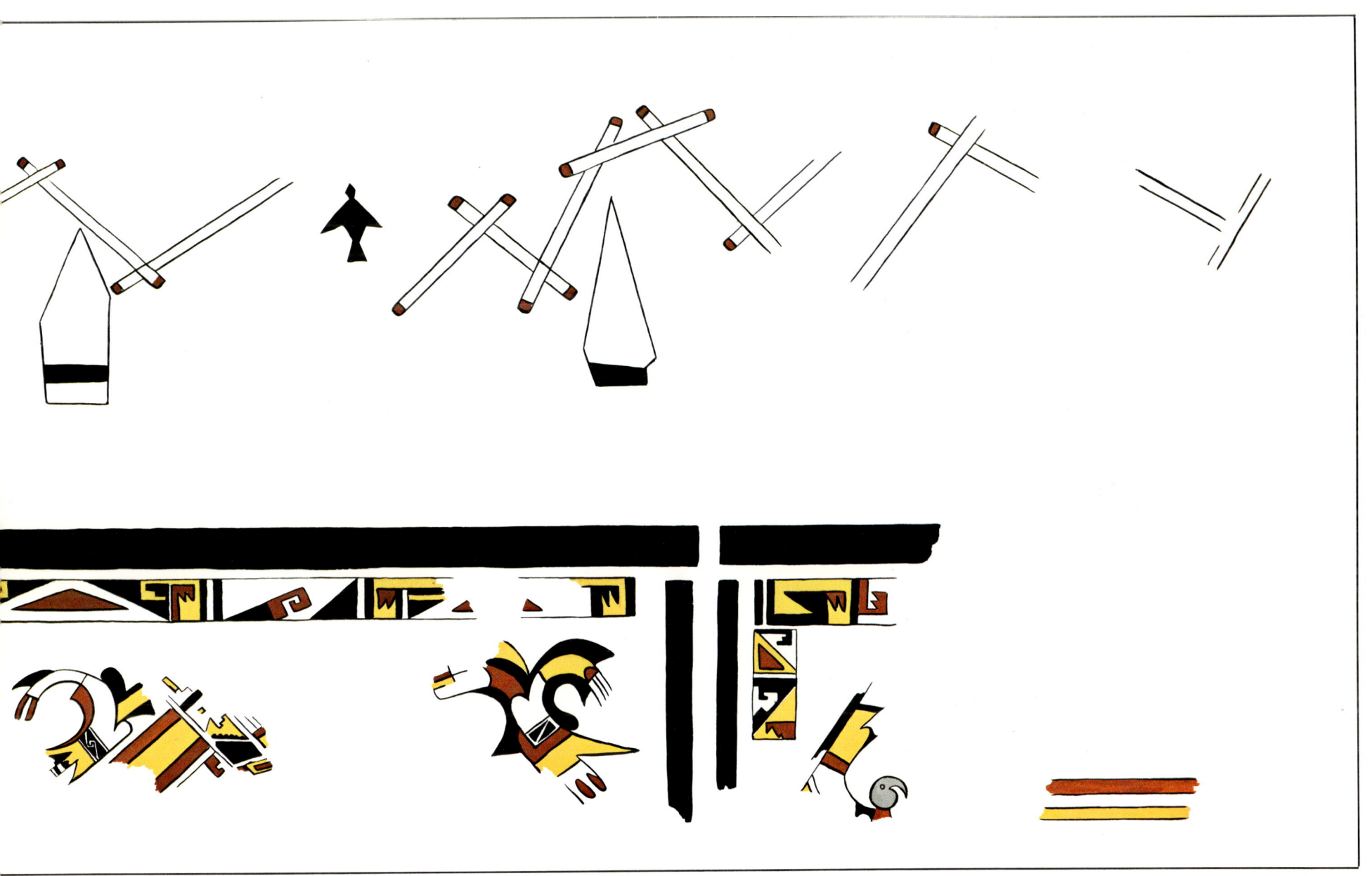

Fig. 108. Ceremonial spears, a pottery vessel, and a bird are interspersed among lightning bolts. A stylized panel appears below. (KIVA 2, LAYER 18, WEST WALL)

CONCLUSION

It is doubtful that another series of Anasazi paintings comparable to those from Pottery Mound will be discovered in the future, although this is a much hoped-for event. At the time of writing, Kiva 17 is being excavated at Pottery Mound. This kiva has multiple layers of paintings, as the other kivas at the site have had. Two other painted kivas are now known and remain as yet unexcavated. Hopefully, archeologists with better techniques for the removal of these precious paintings will be able to carry on the investigations in these kivas in future years. It is also hoped that many people with various interests will contribute their knowledge to investigations of the significance and importance of the Pottery Mound murals. Thus, it is the ultimate aim that in a future edition of this work all of the information left behind by these remarkably creative Anasazi artists will be presented in its entirety.

Fig. 109. Piled-up clouds with a dark center simulate rain clouds. Lightning strokes flash from the thunderhead, and a thunderbird appears at the end of the bolt. (KIVA 8, LAYER 4, SOUTH WALL)

Bibliography

Baerreis, David A. 1957. The Southern Cult and the Spiro Ceremonial Complex. *Oklahoma Anthropological Society Bulletin*, vol. 5.

Bahti, Thomas N. 1949. A Largo-Gallina Pit House and Two Surface Structures. *El Palacio*, vol. 56, no. 2.

_____. 1968. *Southwestern Indian Tribes*. KC Publications, Las Vegas, Nevada.

_____. 1970. *Southwestern Indian Ceremonials*. KC Publications, Las Vegas, Nevada.

Bliss, Wesley L. 1935. Preservation of the Murals of Kiva III, Kuaua Pueblo Ruins. Master's thesis. University of New Mexico, Albuquerque.

_____. 1936. Problems of the Kuaua Mural Paintings. *El Palacio*, vol. 40; nos. 16, 17, 18.

_____. 1948. Preservation of the Kuaua Mural Paintings. *American Antiquity*, vol. 13, no. 3.

Brand, Donald D.; Hawley, Florence M.; Hibben, Frank C. 1937. Tseh So, A Small House Ruin, Chaco Canyon, New Mexico. *University of New Mexico Bulletin 308*. Anthropological Series, vol. 2, no. 2.

Brew, J. O. 1946. Archaeology of Alkali Ridge, Southeastern Utah. *Harvard University Peabody Museum of American Archaeology and Ethnology Papers*, vol. 21.

Bunzel, Ruth L. 1932. Zuni Katcinas. *Bureau of American Ethnology Forty-seventh Annual Report*.

Chapman, Kenneth. 1916. The Cave Pictographs of the Rito de los Frijoles. *New Mexico Archaeological Institute of America, School of American Archaeology Papers*, no. 37.

_____. 1927. A Feather Symbol of the Ancient Pueblos. *El Palacio*, vol. 23, no. 21.

_____. 1938. Pajaritan Pictography: Cave Pictographs of the Rito de los Frijoles. In Hewett, 1938. Pajarito Plateau and its Ancient People. Appendix I, *Handbooks of Archaeological History*.

Dibble, L. E.   Personal communication.

DiPeso, Charles C. 1968. *Casas Grandes and the Gran Chichimeca*. Museum of New Mexico Press, Santa Fe.

_____. 1974. *Casas Grandes*. Northland Press, Flagstaff, Arizona.

Dutton, Bertha P. 1963. *Sun Father's Way: The Kiva Murals of Kuaua*. University of New Mexico Press, Albuquerque.

Ellis, Bruce T. 1956. A Possible Chain Mail Fragment from Pottery Mound. *El Palacio*, vol. 62.

Ellis, Florence M. 1936. Field Manual of Southwestern Pottery Types. *University of New Mexico Bulletin 291*. Anthropological Series, vol. 1, no. 4.

Fewkes, J. Walter. 1917. A Prehistoric Mesa Verde Pueblo and Its People. *Smithsonian Institution Annual Report, 1916*.

Hargrave, Lyndon L. 1933. The Museum of Northern Arizona Archaeological Expedition, Wupatki National Monument. *Museum of Northern Arizona Museum Notes*, vol. 6, no. 5.

_____. 1970. Mexican Macaws. Comparative Osteology and Survey of Remains from the Southwest. *University of Arizona Anthropological Papers*, no. 20.

Hayden, Julian. 1940. Excavations at the University Indian Ruin. *Southwest Monuments Association Technical Series*, vol. 5.

Hibben, Frank C. 1937. Excavation of the Riana Ruin and the Chama Valley Survey. *University of New Mexico Bulletin 300*. Anthropological Series, vol. 2.

_____. 1955. Excavations at Pottery Mound, New Mexico. *American Antiquity*, vol. 21, no. 2.

_____. 1960. Prehispanic Murals of Pottery Mound, New Mexico. *Archaeology*, vol. 13, no. 4.

_____. 1961. The Dating of Pottery Mound, New Mexico. Chapter on archaeology in *Illustrated World History*. George Rainbird, Ltd., London.

_____. 1966. A Possible Pyramidal Structure and Other Mexican Influences at Pottery Mound, New Mexico. *American Antiquity*, vol. 31, no. 4.

_____. 1967. Mexican Features of Mural Paintings at Pottery Mound, New Mexico. *Archaeology*, vol. 20, no. 2.

Hodge, Frederick W. 1922. Recent Excavations at Hawikuh. *El Palacio*, vol. 12, no. 1.

Jeancon, J. A. 1923. Excavations in the Chama Valley, New Mexico. *Bureau of American Ethnology Bulletin 81*.

Judd, Neil M. 1964. The Architecture of Pueblo Bonito. *Smithsonian Miscellaneous Collections*, vol. 147, no. 1.

Kent, K. P. 1957. The Cultivation and Weaving of Cotton in the Prehistoric Southwestern United States. *American Philosophical Society Transactions*, vol. 47, pt. 3.

Kidder, Alfred V. Personal communication.

Martin, Paul S. 1936. Lowry Ruin in Southwestern Colorado. *Field Museum of Natural History Anthropological Publications*.

Matthews, Washington. 1902. The Night Chant, a Navaho Ceremony. *American Museum of Natural History Memoirs*. Anthropological Series, vol. 5.

Mindeleff, Cosmos. 1897. The Cliff Ruins of Canyon de Chelly, Arizona. *Bureau of American Ethnology Sixteenth Annual Report*.

Morris, Earl H. 1924. The Aztec Ruin Annex. *American Museum of Natural History Anthropological Papers*, vol. 26, pt. 4.

Nordenskiold, Gustav. 1893. *The Cliff Dwellers of the Mesa Verde, Southwestern Colorado: Their Pottery and Implements*. Translated by D. Lloyd Morgan. Stockholm.

Parsons, Elsie Clews. 1926. The Ceremonial Calendar of the Tewa of Arizona. *American Anthropologist*, vol. 28, no. 1.

Pepper, George H. 1920. Pueblo Bonito. *American Museum of Natural History Anthropological Papers*, vol. 27.

Prudden, T. M. 1914. The Circular Kivas of Small Ruins in the San Juan Watershed. *American Anthropologist*, vol. 16, no. 1.

———. 1918. A Further Study of Small House Ruins in the San Juan Watershed. *American Anthropological Association Memoirs*, vol. 5, no. 1.

Reagan, Albert B. 1917. The Jemez Indians. *El Palacio*, vol. 4, no. 2.

Schaafsma, Polly and Curtis. 1974. Evidence for the Origins of Pueblo Katchina Cult as Suggested by Rock Art. *American Antiquity*, vol. 39, no. 4.

Schroeder, Albert H. 1965. Unregulated Diffusion from Mexico into the Southwest Prior to A.D. 700. *American Antiquity*, vol. 30, no. 3.

Smith, Watson. 1952. Kiva Mural Decorations at Awatovi and Kawaikaa. *Harvard University Peabody Museum of American Archaeology and Ethnology Papers*, vol. 37. Cambridge.

Spier, Leslie A. 1932. Havasupai Ethnology. *American Museum of Natural History Anthropological Papers*, vol. 29.

Stephen, Alexander M. 1936. Hopi Journal of Alexander M. Stephen. Edited by Elsie Clews Parsons. *Columbia University Contributions to Anthropology*, vol. 23.

Stevenson, Tilly E. 1915. Ethnobotany of the Zuni Indians. *Bureau of American Ethnology Thirtieth Annual Report*.

Stirling, Matthew W. 1942. Origin Myths of Acoma and Other Records. *Bureau of American Ethnology Bulletin 135*.

Tichy, Marjorie F. 1938. The Kivas of Paako and Kuaua. *New Mexico Anthropologist*, vol. 2.

Villágra, Gaspar Perez de. 1610. *Historia de la Nueva Mexico*. Seville. Reprinted 1900 in Mexico. Edited by Luis Gonzalez Obregon. Translated in Espinosa, 1933.

Vivian, Gordon. 1935. Frescoes Uncovered at Kuaua. *El Palacio*, vol. 38; nos. 9, 10, 11.

Voll, Charles. 1961. The Glaze Paint Ceramics of Pottery Mound. Master's thesis. University of New Mexico, Albuquerque.

Wasley, William W. 1960. A Hohokam Platform at the Gatlin Site, Gila Bend, Arizona. *American Antiquity*, vol. 26, no. 2.

Wetherill, Richard. 1894. No title. *The Archaeologist*, vol. 2, no. 10.

White, Leslie A. 1932. The Acoma Indians. *Bureau of American Ethnology Forty-seventh Annual Report*.

Wormington, H. Marie. 1947. *Prehistoric Indians of the Southwest*. Denver Museum of Natural History Popular Series, no. 7.

Kiva Index

This index is provided for those who wish to compare the art work from a given kiva or layer within a kiva. References are to pages on which the figures appear.

Kiva 1
Layer 1: 15, 82, 101, 120, 121
Layer 3: 25
Layer 4: 70

Kiva 2
Layer 1: 26-27, 32-33, 68-69
Layer 2: 36, 55, 106-107, 119
Layer 3: 131, 132, 133
Layer 4: 3, 31, 45, 120
Layer 7: 17(2)
Layer 8: 56, 57
Layer 9 or 10: 47
Layer 11: 35
Layer 11 or 12: 112
Layer 13: 83
Layer 14: 90-91
Layer 16: 112
Layer 18: 136-137

Kiva 6
Layer 1: 66, 67, 135(2)
Layer 10: 75

Kiva 7
Layer 1: 85
Layer 3: 44

Layer 4: 114
Layer 6: 126
Layer 9: 9, 48
Layer 10: 64-65, 115
Layer 11: 109
Layer 14: 127
Layer 18: 45, 49
Layer 21: 111, 113
Layer 26?: 114
Layer 30: 19, 50, 53, 84
Layer 31: 45, 98
Layer 33: 1, 51
Layer 34: 5
Layer 35: 74, 77

Kiva 8
Layer 1: 22-23, 76, 96, 104, 105
Layer 3: 81, 118
Layer 4: 44, 138
Layer 5: 60, 103
Layer 6: 80, 116
Layer 7: 134
Layer 8: 29
Layer 11: 13
Layer 14: 46
Layer 15: 42, 43

Layer 16: 40
Layer 20: 72-73, 86, 87

Kiva 9
Layer 1: 72-73, 86, 87
Layer 2: 62-63, 78-79
Layer 3: 94, 95, 117
Layer 8: 58-59
Layer 12: 130

Kiva 10
Layer 4: 38
Layer 5: 37
Layer 10: 124
Layer 29: 61
Layer 31: 5, 11

Kiva 12
Layer 25: 125

Kiva 16
Layer 1: 128, 29
Layer 3: 71, 99
Layer 4: 108, 110
Layer 9: 39
Layer 11: 41, 122-123

Figure Index

This index includes pages on which figures appear (boldface) and pages on which figures are referred to in text matter (roman).

Title page: 28, 65, 80, 88, 102, 104, 109, 121
Fig. 1: **1**, 94, 117
Fig. 2: **3**, 104, 117
Fig. 3: **5**, 81
Fig. 4: 2, **5**
Fig. 5: **9**, 28, 104
Fig. 6: **11**, 67
Fig. 7: 12, **13**, 43, 102
Fig. 8: **15**, 16, 24, 43, 50, 88, 115, 117, 136
Fig. 9: **17**, 118
Fig. 10: **17**, 118
Fig. 11: **19**, 118
Fig. 12: **22-23**, 39, 136
Fig. 13: 24, **25**, 67
Fig. 14: **26-27**, 28, 48, 67, 78, 80, 81, 88, 94, 102, 126, 134
Fig. 15: 28, **29**
Fig. 16: 28, **31**, 121
Fig. 17: 18, 28, **32-33**, 67, 78, 80, 81, 94, 96, 113, 124
Fig. 18: 28, **35**, 42, 63, 80
Fig. 19: **36**, 38
Fig. 20: **37**, 38, 113
Fig. 21: **38**, 38, 67
Fig. 22: **39**, 39, 67
Fig. 23: **40**, 40, 78
Fig. 24: 24, 39, **41**, 78
Fig. 25: 40, **42**, 93
Fig. 26: 40, **43**, 93
Fig. 27: 42, **44**, 80
Fig. 28: 42, **44**, 130
Fig. 29: 42, **45**, 80
Fig. 30: 24, 42, **45**, 122
Fig. 31: 43, **45**, 88, 117
Fig. 32: 43, **46**
Fig. 33: 39, 43, **47**, 111
Fig. 34: 46, **48**, 59, 134
Fig. 35: 46, **49**, 134

Fig. 36: 48, **50**, 67
Fig. 37: 46, 48, **51**, 88, 136
Fig. 38: **53**, 56, 122
Fig. 39: **55**, 56
Fig. 40: **56**, 56
Fig. 41: 39, 56, **57**
Fig. 42: **58-59**, 59, 115
Fig. 43: 59, **60**
Fig. 44: **60**, **61**
Fig. 45: 60, **62-63**, 115, 121, 136
Fig. 46: 63, **64-65**
Fig. 47: 65, **66**, 94, 110
Fig. 48: 65, **67**, 113
Fig. 49: 28, 67, **68-69**, 78, 80, 81, 88, 107, 113, 121, 126
Fig. 50: 67, **70**, 70
Fig. 51: 67, **71**
Fig. 52: 67, 70, **72-73**
Fig. 53: 67, **74**, 74
Fig. 54: 67, 74, **75**
Fig. 55: 74, **76**
Fig. 56: 74, **77**, 111
Fig. 57: 78, **78-79**, 81
Fig. 58: **80**, 88, 118
Fig. 59: 48, **81**
Fig. 60: 24, 81, **82**, 102
Fig. 61: **83**, 88, 136
Fig. 62: 56, **84**, 88, 122
Fig. 63: 78, **85**, 88
Fig. 64: **86**, 121
Fig. 65: 78, 80, **87**, 121
Fig. 66: 78, 88-93, **90-91**
Fig. 67: 42, 78, **94**
Fig. 68: 94, **95**
Fig. 69: **96**, 96, 117
Fig. 70: 63, **98**
Fig. 71: **99**, 100, 122
Fig. 72: 6, 24, 78, 88, **101**, 101, 121, 124

Fig. 73: 102, **103**
Fig. 74: **104**, 105, 121
Fig. 75: 80, **105**, 105, 121
Fig. 76: 28, 80, **106-107**, 117, 122
Fig. 77: **108**, 109
Fig. 78: 107, **109**
Fig. 79: 109, **110**
Fig. 80: 40, **111**
Fig. 81: 88, 111, **112**, 113
Fig. 82: **112**, 115
Fig. 83: 80, **113**
Fig. 84: **114**, 115
Fig. 85: **114**, 115
Fig. 86: **115**, 115
Fig. 87: **116**, 118
Fig. 88: **117**, 117
Fig. 89: **118**, 118
Fig. 90: 118, **119**
Fig. 91: **120**, 121
Fig. 92: **120**, 121
Fig. 93: **121**, 121
Fig. 94: **122-123**, 123
Fig. 95: 123, **124**
Fig. 96: 43, 123, 124, **125**
Fig. 97: **126**, 130
Fig. 98: 40, 60, 126, **127**
Fig. 99: 80, 121, 126, **128**
Fig. 100: 80, 121, 126, **129**
Fig. 101: 7, 65, **130**, 130
Fig. 102: 28, 65, 130, **131**
Fig. 103: 28, 65, **132**, 139
Fig. 104: 28, 65, 130, **133**
Fig. 105: **134**, 134
Fig. 106: 134, **135**
Fig. 107: 134, **135**
Fig. 108: 136, **136-137**
Fig. 109: 136, **138**

General Index

This index contains references to text matter (roman) and captions for illustrations (italic). It is not intended to include a complete listing of all elements present in the murals themselves.

Abstract designs, 11, 25, 38, 39, 40, 49, 50, 67, 70, 70-74, 71, 75, 136, 137
Acoma: pueblo, 54, 93, 111; *information:* "butterfly maiden," 86, 87; constellations, 82; "creation" scene, 14, 115; "direction men," 56, 56; "dragonfly man," 114, 115; feather usage, 97; "man in the moon," 74, 76; mountain lion, 109; "mosquito man," 63, 115; paints, 50; prayer sticks, 36, 100; "soul faces," 48, 134, 134, 135; "squash head," 45; textile designs, 121; tiponis, 104; "two aspects of mankind," 80, 116
Altars, 20, 67, 67
Anasazi: agriculture, xi, xii; civilization, xi-xiii; clothing and textiles, 120-126; marriage, 12, 40; modern application of term, xii; representations of selves, 3, 31, 45, 63, 67, 67, 78, 80, 85, 104, 128-129. *See also* Architecture; Ceremonialism
Animals, 107-113. *See also* Bear; Jaguar; Mountain lion
Antelope, 112, 113; "man," 54
Apache, 93
Architecture, Pottery Mound, xii, xiii, 4, 6, 8, 10, 11, 21. *See also* Kivas
Arm and leg decorations, 88, 101, 121
Art reproductions of murals, 6, 7, 14
Art techniques used in murals, 24, 28, 36-50, 70, 101. *See also* Abstract designs; Human figures; Superimposition
Aspergilla, 104, 104, 105
Atlatl, 70, 130, 131
Awatovi, xi, 12, 30, 70, 96, 97

Baerreis, David A., 60
Bahti, Thomas N., xii, 30, 118
Ball courts, xii, 10, 59, 60

Bandoleer, 7, 88, 101
Banners, 85
Banquettes in kivas, 6, 18, 20, 20
Basketmakers, xii, 4
Basketry and baskets, 31, 45, 126, 126-129, 136
Baton, 5, 25, 54, 81
Bead strings, 17, 31. *See also* Necklaces; Shells
Bear, 46, 111; in Acoma and Zuni usage, 111; "man," 106; tallow as binder, 49
Bells, as decoration, 88
Belts, 94
Binder, paint, 36, 49-50
Bird: headdresses, 81; "men," 106; representations, 1, 44, 50, 53, 94, 137; scepter, 25; staffs, 81, 82; thunder-, 138; tracks, 96. *See also* Eagle; Feathers; Parrots; Whooping crane
Birds and feathers, 93-102
Blackbird feathers, 97, 101
Blankets, Anasazi, 31, 120-125, 122-125
Bluebird feathers, 97, 102
Bliss, Wesley L., 14
Body-painting, 42, 43, 78, 81, 82, 94
Bow and arrows, 44, 46, 67, 80, 88, 131
Brand, Donald D., et al., 30
Brew, J. O., 30
Bunzel, Ruth L., 96
Burials: of macaws, 8, 64; human, 21
"Butterfly maiden," 86, 87

Caliche, 8, 10
Casas Grandes, 8, 10, 11, 60, 64
Catholic: churchmen, 89, 92; missions, 92
Ceramics. *See* Pottery
Ceremonialism: architecture as related to, 8, 11; eagle-jaguar cult, 65, 110; hunting, 107, 113; modern Pueblo, 34, 88, 96, 97, 100, 101, 102, 104, 110, 111, 113, 115, 118, 130, 134, 136; paraphernalia of, 5, 22, 31, 67, 88, 93-105, 136. *See also* Kachina cult; Kivas; Mexican influences; Parrots; Rain; Rainmaking; Spirit figures
Chat, 96; feathers, 97
Chino family of Acoma, 54, 109
Chapman, Kenneth, 97
Clark, John: color analyses of, 38-50
Clothing, Anasazi, 45, 120-126. *See also* Kilts
Clouds and cloud symbols, 1, 50, 83, 136, 138. *See also* Lightning; Rain; Rainmaking
Clubs, 7, 67, 88
Color matching. *See* Art reproduction
Color: shading, 24, 36; superimposition, 24, 39, 40
Colors: used in murals, 24, 36-50; background, 24, 49; moiety, 12, 78
Composite figures, 14, 19, 45, 80, 96, 116, 117, 118. *See also* Zoomorphs
Constellations, 82
Corn Mother, 104
Corn: plants, 53, 70, 71, 114, 128; -stalk staff, 31
Coronado, xi, 4, 12, 89
Cosmos, 74, 74
Cougar. *See* Mountain lion
Council: of chiefs, 25; "of the mountain lions," 65, 67, 109; of war, 65
Coyote, 107, 111, 111
"Creation" scene, 14, 16, 115
Crow, 101; feathers, 97, 100

Dating: by pottery, 4; tree-ring, 2, 10, 11-12. *See also* Pottery Mound
Death: associated with raven, 100; depiction of, 67, 67; mask, 130; southern death cult, 60. *See also* Spirit figures
Deer, 113

143

Defacement of murals, 16, 18
Deflector, draft, in kivas, xiii, 6, 18, 20, 22
Design panels. See Abstract designs
Destruction of kiva walls, 16
DiPeso, Charles C., 64
Direction: indicators, 105; "men," 56, symbols, 56, 56, 96
Dragonfly: 53, 59, 63, 71, 114, 115; "man," 114, 115
Ducks, 94; feathers, 97, 101
Dutton, Bertha P., 12, 30

Eagle, 8, 54, 94, 94; -capturing ceremony, 98, 100; feathers, 97, 100, 102, 105; headdress, 102; "man," 5, 28, 54
Eagle-jaguar cult, 65, 110
Earrings, feathered, 81
Effigies, xi; animal, 112, 113. See also Ceremonialism; Kachina cult
Ellis, Bruce T., 4
Ellis, Florence, 10
Entrance hatchways in kivas, xiii, 18
Excavations: at Pottery Mound, xi, 4, 6, 6, 7, 12, 21, 138; at other sites 2, 30, 64. See also Awatovi; Casas Grandes; Hawikuh; Kawaika-a; Kuaua; Wupatki

Face-painting, 44, 78, 78, 80, 81, 110, 120
Fading, of mural colors, 7, 14, 92, 105
Feathered serpent. See Serpent
Feathers, 30, 39, 70, 71, 100, 110, and birds, 93-102; prayer sticks and tiponis, 102-105. See also Earrings; Headdresses; Parrots; Ruffs; Shields; Staffs; Tablitas
Fewkes, J. Walter, 30
Firepits in kivas, xiii, 6, 18, 20, 22
Floors in kivas, 6, 18, 20
Fox, 107, 111
Framing lines, 3, 28, 34, 56, 60, 63, 98, 134
Frescoes. See Paintings
Fresco secco, 24

Garrote, 89, 93
Ghosts. See Spirit figures
Glazeware. See Pottery
Grafitti, 16, 18
Ground line, 28

Hair styles: Anasazi, 80; non-Anasazi, 78

Hargrave, Lyndon L., 64
Hats, 126
Hawikuh, 30, 89
Hawk feathers, 97, 102
Hawley, Florence M., 30
Headdresses, 25, 31, 53, 67, 81, 81; feathered, 50, 67, 102, 104, 105, 115, 134; horned, 78, 94, 113; moon, 120; rattlesnake, 76
Hibben, Frank C., 18, 30
Hodge, Frederick W., 30
Hohokam, xii, 8, 59
Hopi, 2, 12, 30, 34, 74, 96, 100, 101
Human: figures, 78-88; viscera, 56. See also Composite figures
Hunting societies: at Acoma, 111, at Zuni, 109. See also Ceremonialism

Incising, as art technique, 24, 101, 126
Indians, non-Anasazi, 42, 78, 78, 88, 89, 93, 94
Insect figures, 14, 115; necklaces on, 88

Jaguar, 65, 67, 110-111. See also Eagle-jaguar cult
Jay, 96; feathers, 102
Judd, Neil M., 64

Kachina: costumes, 100, 107, 111; cult, xi, xii, 59, 63, 80, 118; katsina, as term, xi
Kawaika-a, 12, 30, 96
Kuaua, 12, 14, 30
Kent, K. P., xi, 120
Kilts, 36, 45, 87, 101, 120, 121, 121-124; feathered, 42, 43, 93; non-Anasazi, 40, 78
Kivas: alterations of, 16, 22, 24; architectural features of, xii-xiii, 6, 16, 18, 20, 20, 22, 31, 54, 81; construction of, xii, 12, 14, 18; interiors of, 31, 67, 81; orientation of, 18, 21; Spanish term for, xiii; superimposition of, 24. See also Plaster layers
Kiva-step design, 1, 20, 70, 71, 124, 136

Laguna, 54, 100
Lienzo Tlaxcala, 65
Lightning symbols, 23, 63, 83, 136, 137, 138
Loom holes in kivas, 20, 22

Macaw, 94, 96, 97; burials; 8, 64. See also Birds; Feathers; Parrots
Magpie feathers, 97, 102

Mammals, 107-113; necklaces on, 88
Manta, 121
Marriage among Anasazi, 12, 40
Martin, Paul S., 30
Masks and masked figures, 17, 34, 36, 45, 63, 64, 67, 76, 80-81, 83, 113, 118, 130
Matthews, Washington, 34
Medallions, 23, 74, 74, 76, 77, 83
Medicine-society: kivas, 12, 14, 54; ritual, 104
Mexican codices, 65, 74
Mexican influences, xii, 8, 10, 59-67, 74, 97, 110, 115, 126, 126, 130, 130, 133. See also Birds and feathers; Ceremonialism; Parrots; Shields
Minerals used in paints, 36-49
Missions, Spanish, 92-93
Moiety: colors, 12, 78; kivas, 12, 14
Moon: headdress, 120; "man in the —," 74, 76
Mosquito, 115; "man," 63, 115, 115
Mountain lion, 8, 44, 107, 109, 109; council of the, 65, 67, 109; quivers, 107, 110
Murals, Pottery Mound: colors used in, 24, 36-50; physical aspects of, 24; removal techniques of, 14; wear and repair of, 16. See also Art reproductions of murals; Art techniques used in murals
Musculature in human figures, 78

Nampeyo, 74
Navajo: art, xi, xii; sandpainting, xi, 34, 134; weaving, xi, 120, 123, 124
Necklaces, 34, 45, 53, 84, 85, 88, 112. See also Shells
Netting, 126, 126
Niches in kiva walls, 20, 54

Obliteration, of paintings. See Plaster layers
Oñate, 34, 54, 89, 92
Organic elements in paints, 43, 46, 49-50
Owl feathers, 97, 102

Pahos, 102, 104
Painting: body-, 42, 43; face-, 44, 78
Paintings, Pottery Mound, See Murals
Paints used in murals, 36-50
"Parrot ladies," 56
Parrots, 31, 34, 54, 60-64, 63, 64, 86, 87, 97, 98, 101, 106; as live birds, 60, 63-64, 126; as Mexican influence, 8, 60; stylized depictions of, 25,

39, 53, 70, 71, 75, 121, 122. *See also* Birds; Feathers
Parsons, Elsie Clews, 100
Petroglyphs and pictographs, xiii, 80
Photographs at site, *6, 7,* 14, *92, 98, 105, 115*
Pigments used in paintings, 24, 36-50
Pithouses, xii, xiii
Plaster: jacketing of fragments, 14, 16; layers, 12, 14, 16, 22, 24, 28, 30, 34; preparation of, 24
Pottery, 2, 4, *5,* 60, *63,* 136, *137*. *See also* Dating; Sikyatki elements
Pottery Mound: cultural affiliations, 2, 8; dating, xii, 4, 10, 88-93; site, xi, 2, 10-11, *21*, 93, 138. *See also* Architecture; Ceremonialism; Excavations; Kivas; Mexican influences; Murals; Pottery
Prayer plumes, *12, 31, 82,* 100, 101
Prayer sticks, 102, 104, 118
Priest, "Spanish," painting, 88-93
Pueblo ceremonialism. *See* Ceremonialism
Pueblo culture periods, 4
Pueblo Revolt, 89, 93
Pueblo towns and sites, xi, xii, 2, 30, 64; Acoma, 54, 93; Isleta, 89; Laguna, 54, 100; Piro, Tigua, 89, 92; Sia, 34, 50; Walpi, 34. *See also* Acoma; Excavations; Hopi; Rio Grande pueblos; Zuni
Puerco Valley, 2, 10-11, 93
Puma. *See* Mountain lion
Pyramidal substructure at Pottery Mound, xii, 4, 6, 8, 10, 11, *21*

Quetzal, 94; feathers, 97, 101
Quetzalcoatl, 115
Quivers, 65, *67, 76,* 88; of mountain-lion skin, 107, *110*

Racks, *5*. *See also* Shelves
Rain: petitions for, 96, *134*; symbols of, *37, 63,* 100, 113, 115. *See also* Clouds; Lightning; Rainmaking
Rainbow: *40, 134*; "man," *25,* 81, *134*; motif, 74, 77. *See also* Framing lines
Rainmaking, *63, 71,* 94, 96, 97, 104, 105, *105,* 113. *See also* Clouds; Lightning; Rain
Rattles, 88, *128*
Rattlesnake, *28, 37, 40, 109,* 113, *134*; headdresses *76,* 81; staffs, *67,* 81

Raven, *101*; feathers, 97, 100
Reagan, Albert B., 34
Removal of murals, 14
Reptiles, *112*, 113-114
Rio Grande pueblos, xii, 2, 4, 8, 12
Rituals and ritual paraphernalia. *See* Ceremonialism
Roadrunner, 101; feathers, 97, 101, *102*
Rohona, 111. *See also* Jaguar
Rooms at Pottery Mound, 4, 6, 8, *21*
Ruffs, feathered, *23, 59, 134, 135*

Sandpainting, xi, 34, 56, 136; Havasupai, 34; Navajo, xi, 34, 134
Sashes, 121
Scepters, *25, 54,* 81
Schaffsma, Polly and Curtis, 81
Schroeder, Albert H., 8, 59
Serpent, horned and feathered (plumed), 40, *48, 59, 59,* 113, *113,* 134. *See also* Snakes and reptiles
Shading, as art technique, 24, 36
Shells, *34, 53,* 60, *84,* 88. *See also* Necklaces
Shelves and racks in kivas, *31, 67,* 80-81, *122*
Shields, *31,* 44, 46, 65, *67, 109, 126,* 130, *130-133*
Shirts, *45,* 98, 123
Sikyatki elements, *11, 39, 50, 70, 71, 74*. *See also* Pueblo sites
Sipapu, xiii, *20,* 22
Skin colors, 42, 78
Skunk, 74, *77,* 111
Smith, Watson, 12, 30, 70, 96
Smoke-blackening of kivas, 22, 24, 30
Snake: dance, 100; skins, 113, 121
Snakes and reptiles, 113-114. *See also* Rattlesnakes; Serpent
"Soul faces," *48,* 134, *134, 135*
Spanish: conquistadores, xi, xii, 4, 12, 89; friars, 92; historical records, 34, 89-93; missions, 92-93; "priest" painting, 88-93, *89, 92*
Spears, 78, 81, 88, *130*; ceremonial, *25, 83,* 88, *137*
Spier, Leslie A., 34
Spirit: faces, 134, *134-135*; figures, *19, 36, 106, 118, 118, 119*; masks, *17, 64*; voice, 44
Spirits. *See* Ceremonialism; Kachina cult
"Spotted ladies," 56, *84*

Squash: "head," *45*; "maiden," *106*; moiety, 12, 78
Staffs, 81, *121*; bird-decorated, *82*; cornstalk, *31*; feathered, *12, 34, 42, 43, 56, 67, 83,* 94
Stairs. *See* Architecture, Pottery Mound
Stars, *43, 48, 49, 74, 74, 134, 135*
Stephen, Alexander M., 34, 96, 101, 126
Stevenson, Tilly E., 96
Stirling, Matthew W., 97, 111
Stylized elements. *See* Abstract designs
Superimposition: of colors, 24, 39, 40; of elements, 28, *28, 48, 109*; of kivas, 24
Swallow, 94, 96, *96*; feathers, 97

Tables (information), 4, 16, 30
Tablitas, 59, *86, 87*
Tassels, *36, 40, 120,* 121
Textiles, 120-126. *See also* Blankets; Clothing; Kilts
Thunderbird, *138*
Tiponis, *8, 77,* 104
Trousers, *115,* 123
Tunnels in kivas, 16, 18, 20, *31*
Turkey feathers, 97, 100, 105
Turquoise: color, 43, 46; moiety, 12, 78

Varves, 30, 34. *See also* Smoke-blackening
Ventilators in kivas, xiii, *6,* 18, *20,* 22
Villágra, Gaspar Perez de, 34
Vivian, Gordon, 4, 30
Voll, Charles, xiii

Warriors, *7, 76,* 80, 130, *130-133*
War societies, 65, 109, 130
Wasley, William W., 8
Weaving: Anasazi, xi, 120-126; Navajo, xi, 120, 123, 124, *124*
White, Leslie A., 36
Whitewash: as background, 24, 28; as ceremonial routine, 34
Whooping crane, *31,* 96
Wolf, 107, 109-110, *110*
Woodpecker feathers, 97, 102
Wormington, H. Marie, xii, 74
Wupatki, 8, 64

Zoomorphs, *3, 23, 40, 54,* 88, *96, 106,* 114, 115, *115,* 117, *117*
Zuni, 89, 93, 96, 109, 111

145

Kiva Art of the Anasazi
DESIGNED BY K. C. DEN DOOVEN
SET IN HANOVER BY NEVADA GRAPHICS
PRINTED BY W. A. KRUEGER COMPANY
ON KARMA TEXT MADE BY POTLATCH CORPORATION
BOUND BY ROSWELL BINDERY
COLOR SEPARATIONS BY NORTHLAND PRESS